Reflections on Revolutions

Reflections on Revolutions

Mark N. Katz

St. Martin's Press
New York

ISBN 0-312-22356-0 (cloth)

Library of Congress Cataloging-in-Publication Data
Katz, Mark N.
    Reflections on revolutions / Mark N. Katz.
        p. cm.
    Includes bibliographical references.
    ISBN 0-312-22356-0 (cloth)
    1. Revolutions. I. Title.
JC491.K284 1999
303.6'4—dc21   99–20613
                                                                  CIP

Design by Letra Libre, Inc.

First edition: September, 1999
10 9 8 7 6 5 4 3 2 1

To Melissa and Her Mom

CONTENTS

Acknowledgements

I WOULD LIKE TO EXPRESS MY GRATITUDE to Patrick Conge, Adeed Dawisha, Dale Eickelman, Francis Fukuyama, Walter Goldfrank, Jack Goldstone, Jeff Goodwin, Liah Greenfeld, Ted Robert Gurr, Andrew Katz, Torbjørn Knutsen, Cynthia McClintock, James Pfiffner, Eric Selbin, Jennifer Taw, and Timothy Wickham-Crowley for their comments, suggestions, and encouragement at various stages of this project. I would also like to thank Kannan P. Selvaratnam for the research assistance he provided during the summer of 1997. Special thanks are due to my wife, Nancy Yinger, both for her general support and for composing Figure 1 for me.

Chapter 2 was originally presented at the International Studies Association-West conference on October 18, 1997, in Davis, California. It also appeared in a somewhat different form in *Studies in Conflict and Terrorism*. Chapter 4 was originally presented at the International Studies Association annual convention in Minneapolis, Minnesota, on March 21, 1998. Chapter 6 was originally presented at the International Studies Association annual convention in Washington, D.C., on February 20, 1999. Chapter 3 was originally presented at the American Political Science Association annual meeting in Atlanta, Georgia, on September 3, 1999.

This book was written with the support of a fellowship research grant from the Earhart Foundation and a sabbatical from George Mason University.

THINKING METAPHORICALLY ABOUT REVOLUTION

Reflections on Crane Brinton

REASONING BY ANALOGY APPEARS to be an old-fashioned method of trying to understand revolution, or any topic within the social sciences. Today, social scientists want to find the actual causes of events, not metaphors for them. But reasoning by analogy can often reveal important insights about a subject, and perhaps more important, how it is studied.

Reasoning by analogy was the hallmark of one of the classic books on revolution, Crane Brinton's *The Anatomy of Revolution* (1965), which was originally published in 1938. In it, Brinton compared the course of revolution to the course of fever. In this chapter, I will discuss the strengths and weaknesses of Brinton's theory of revolution over 60 years after it was first published. I will then examine what I think is a better metaphor for revolution: murder. I will also discuss how several of the most prominent theories about the causes of revolution can be seen as variations on the elements that make up murder: motive, means, and opportunity.

Brinton published the first edition of *The Anatomy of Revolution* in 1938, the second edition in 1952, and the third edition in 1965. Later theorists of revolution, however, have tended to distance themselves from, dismiss, or simply ignore Brinton. In her highly influential *States and Social Revolutions*, Theda Skocpol described Brinton's method as "natural history" and her own as "comparative historical analysis." She noted that

> At first glance, comparative historical analysis may not seem so very different from the approach of the "natural historians" . . . They, too, analyzed and compared a few historical cases in depth. Actually, however, comparative-historical and natural-history approaches to revolutions differ both in objective and in method of analysis. Whereas the goal of comparative historical analysis is to establish causes of revolutions, the natural historians sought to describe the characteristic cycle, or sequence of stages, that should typically occur in the processes of revolutions. (1979, 37)

In other words, while Skocpol sought to explain why revolution occurred, Brinton merely described how it did so. Ted Robert Gurr wrote that a "fundamental limitation" of most "older" theories of revolution such as Brinton's "was the difficulty of deriving falsifiable hypotheses from them" (1970, 17–18). In his much-quoted division of writers on revolution into three generations, Jack Goldstone placed Brinton in the first generation, whose work was characterized as inductive, descriptive, and taxonomic—which was, by implication, inferior to the historical but analytical and interdisciplinary approach of the third generation (1980). Finally, while Barrington Moore, in his monumental *Social Origins of Dictatorship and Democracy* (1966), examined the same four countries (plus others) that Brinton discussed in *The Anatomy of Revolution*, Brinton does not even appear in Moore's bibliography or index.

Yet despite what later scholars wrote (or did not write) about it, *The Anatomy of Revolution* is still in print and used as a text over 60 years after the first edition was published. And while many of the leading theorists of revolution saw little utility in the book, some leading policymakers assessed it far more positively. Former National Security Adviser Zbigniew Brzezinski cited Brinton as the authority for his view that the Iranian Revolution of 1979 was not inevitable and that "an established leadership . . . could disarm the opposition through a timely combination of repression and concession" (1983, 355). Gary Sick, a member of the National Security Council staff at the time, described the Iranian Revolution as "an almost textbook case" of Brinton's depiction of how a revolution unfolds (1986, 187). Even some of those scholars who dismissed Brinton as "descriptive" then went on to cite him in support of various arguments they made (Gurr 1970, 114, 118, 146, 150, 314; Colburn 1994, 49–50, 96).

Thus, despite the scholarly criticisms leveled against it, *The Anatomy of Revolution* continues to be widely read and cited—even by scholars. What appears to account for this is Brinton's readily comprehensible metaphor for understanding revolution. According to Brinton, the course of a revolution was similar to the course of a fever. The initial stages of a revolution, like fever, were hard to detect. Once the symptoms were visible, it was too late to prevent the fever from developing. For Brinton, though, the downfall of the old regime was not the most feverish stage of the illness. For it was the moderate revolutionaries who first took power. The problems they faced, however, would prove too much for them, and soon the moderate revolutionaries would be discredited and replaced in power by extremists. These extremists would then launch a reign of terror aimed at altering the very nature of mankind. This stage would mark the highest point of the fever. Inevitably, though, the extremists would turn against one another while the population as a whole would lose faith in them. The revolutionary fever would break with the downfall of the extremists and the rise of more moderate rulers who would usher in Thermidor—the period of convalescence and retreat from revolutionary excess. Relapses of revolutionary fever might break out again, but they too would be followed by convalescence and a return to normality. In the end, Brinton suggested, a nation experiencing revolution—like a person experiencing fever—returned to much the same state that they were in beforehand.

What is noteworthy about *The Anatomy of Revolution* is that even though it discusses only four specific cases (the seventeenth-century English, the eighteenth-century American and French, and the early-twentieth-century Russian revolutions), the stages of revolution Brinton outlined appear to be present in many other revolutions as well. Brinton stated that "the revolution in Russia has essentially run its course" (1965, 233), decades before the USSR actually collapsed. And as Sick noted, the unfolding of the Iranian Revolution occurred in a sequence remarkably similar to the stages of revolution described by Brinton.

Thus, while describing how revolution occurs may be far more modest a task then explaining why it occurs, Brinton's continued popularity results from his having performed this task so well. Indeed, Brinton's 1938 depiction of how revolutions occur appears to be far more relevant than many more recent explanations of why they do for contemporary, post–Cold War revolutions.

Nevertheless, there are serious problems with Brinton's fever metaphor. While his depiction of how revolution unfolds applies to many cases, it certainly does not apply to all. Brinton implies that once the symptoms of disease are present, the fever of revolution will follow. But as Timothy Lomperis demonstrates, some revolutions have been halted even after spreading throughout much of a country (1996). When a revolution does succeed in ousting the *ancien régime*, a reign of terror does not inevitably follow. There was, for example, no reign of terror in one of the four cases Brinton examined—the American Revolution. As Knutsen and Bailey pointed out, "Brinton's problems with the American case become obvious towards the middle of the book, when the American Revolution begins to disappear from the discussion" (1989, 429n10). Nor was there a reign of terror following the 1989 democratic revolutions in most of Eastern Europe, or in democratic revolutions generally.

In those cases where there was a reign of terror, a Thermidor following it can usually be identified. Brinton, however, implies that Thermidor is the end of the revolution, marking the beginning of the return to normalcy. But even in the French case—which gave us the term "Thermidor"—things hardly returned to normal, as the rise of Napoleon soon followed. In the Russian case, the New Economic Policy (NEP) period (1922–28) can be considered a Thermidor that followed the terror of the civil war, but NEP was followed by yet another reign of terror under Stalin during the first two five-years plans.

Brinton's metaphor for revolution, then, is too rigid to be applicable to all cases. Indeed, following his own analogy, there are many kinds of diseases. Some are more serious than others. And even those that are serious do not all share the same pathology. Thus, while Brinton provided a useful guide for understanding how a certain type of revolution unfolds, he did not explain how other types unfold—or fail to unfold.

Whatever its flaws, though, coming up with a better metaphor than Brinton's is not an easy task, since such a metaphor must be broad enough to account for the variation in revolutions that Brinton's does not. Is there a better metaphor for revolution than fever? In my view, there is: murder.

There are two ways in which murder and revolution are identical. Just as with those who attempt murder, those who attempt revolution do not always succeed. In addition, just as a successful murderer kills a person, successful revolutionaries destroy a government—or perhaps more accurately, its leadership. Murder and revolution, of course, are not completely identical. A truly successful murderer is able to conceal that he or she killed someone, and has a strong incentive for not revealing what transpired. By contrast, some revolutionaries try to conceal their intention of toppling the ancien régime before actually doing so, but many do not. And once the ancien régime is toppled, revolutionaries—unlike most murderers—immediately claim credit for their actions. This is because, unlike murderers, revolutionaries who topple ancien régimes and set themselves up as *nouveaux régimes* are not likely to be brought to trial. There is, indeed, some irony in comparing revolution to murder, since revolutionaries who fail are likely to be treated as murderers, while revolutionaries who succeed are not.

After "doing the deed," however, all successful revolutionaries do something that many murderers who get caught also do: they claim that they acted out of self-defense, and that their actions should be considered justifiable homicide. Making this argument convincingly is important both for the murderer who has gotten caught and for the revolutionaries who have toppled an ancien régime. The murderer who has gotten caught must make this argument convincingly in order to be acquitted. Successful revolutionaries must do so in order to project the idea that while their overthrow of the ancien régime was justified, any attempt to similarly overthrow their nouveau régime would not be.

The most important similarity between murder and revolution, though, is that in order for either to occur, motive, means, and opportunity must all be present. It is with regard to these three elements in particular that murder is superior to fever as a metaphor for revolution. For while Brinton's fever metaphor implied that there was only one way in which revolution could occur, the murder metaphor has no such implication. Just as there is wide variation in the motives, means, and opportunities that can lead to murder (or attempted murder), there is also wide variation in how these three elements can lead to revolution (or attempted revolution).

Looking at means alone, it is obvious that murder can occur in many possible ways, including shooting, stabbing, strangling, poisoning, smothering, or drowning. Similarly, as I have argued elsewhere, revolution can occur through several means, including rural revolution, urban revolution, coup d'état, revolution "from above," revolution "from without," or a combination of these (Katz 1997, 4–9).

Further, just as all murderers do not share the same motives for killing someone, revolutionaries do not share the same motives for overthrowing an ancien régime. There are many possible motives for murder, including anger, greed, fear, revenge, or even boredom. Similarly, there are many possible motives for revolution, including not just the desire to get rid of whatever ancien régime is in power, but also out of very different visions as to what the nouveau régime should be. Indeed, since revolution is by necessity a group activity, discord can quickly develop among revolutionaries after the ancien régime has been overthrown if they do not share the same vision of the nature of the nouveau régime.

Finally, opportunity can vary considerably from case to case in revolution as well as in murder. In some cases, the would-be perpetrators plan meticulously to create the most favorable opportunity for murder or revolution. In others, however, circumstances outside of their control arise that create the opportunity for murder or revolution that its perpetrators seize upon. And in still other cases, the would-be perpetrators attempt unsuccessfully for years to create the opportunity for murder or revolution, but then unforeseen circumstances arise that make it possible after all.

As this discussion indicates, a wide variety of means, motives, and opportunities can, in different combinations, lead to revolution as well as to murder. And the examples mentioned here by no means exhaust either the possibilities of these three elements or the combinations in which they might occur.

In addition to being useful for thinking about revolution, the murder metaphor is also useful for examining and categorizing theories about and accounts of revolution. Basically, these theories and accounts can be viewed as statements about one or more of the three elements that comprise revolution.

The individual case study—the most basic form of analysis, without which comparative histories and theories would not be possible—examines the means, motives, and opportunities that lead to revolution in a single country. Such studies usually make no attempt to derive any sort of theory or lesson from their particular case that might be applicable to other revolutions. Indeed, the authors of such studies—especially if they are historians—may reject the very notion that theories of revolution apply to their particular revolution, or that their case study can be used to support a more broadly applicable theory of revolution. Just as a murder investigation seeks to explain a single murder and not murder in general, the individual case study seeks to explain a single revolution and not revolution in general. This by itself, it must be emphasized, is no mean feat: determining conclusively the causes either of a single murder or a single revolution can be extremely difficult, if not impossible. And, of course, different investigators may come up with different explanations.

While individual case studies examine the motives, means, and opportunities for a particular revolution, theories that attempt to make a statement about revolution in general based on an examination of several cases tend either to focus on one of these three variables or to see them interacting in a particular way. This can be seen through examining several prominent theories of revolution through the murder metaphor.

In Brinton's *The Anatomy of Revolution,* the victim (ancien régime) is an elderly family tyrant who is no longer in full possession of his faculties, while the perpetrators (revolutionaries) are two adult children still living at home who chafe at how the tyrant rules their lives and who are impatient to inherit the family house and property. The opportunity for murder (revolution) arises when the tyrant becomes so enfeebled that he can no longer defend himself, and the two children band together and kill him. At first, the two children are euphoric. But they have very different characters. One is a rational opportunist (Brinton's moderates) who simply wants to live in peace. The other is a psychopath (Brinton's extremists) who now wants to kill the neighbors and take over their houses (spread revolution abroad). The rational opportunist takes over the management of the house (the moderates take power) at first. But he or she quickly encounters several problems: (1) it turns out that the old man wasn't lying when he told them he had no money to give them; the family (the state) really is bankrupt; (2) the neighbors are horrified at what the two children did to their father, and are fearful about what they might do to them; and (3) the rational opportunist does not realize that his increasingly demanding sibling really is a psychopath until the psychopath overpowers him (the extremists overpower the moderates). The psychopath then makes a complete shambles out of running the household (the reign of terror) and becomes embroiled in bitter disputes with the neighbors, uniting them against him. The psychopath's own actions, however, trip him up, thus allowing the rational opportunist to overpower him and reassert control over the household (Thermidor). The rational opportunist then strikes a bargain with the neighbors: if they won't try to kick him out of his house, he won't try to kick them out of theirs, and so life begins to return to normal.

Brinton's theory of revolution, then, focuses on the motives of the revolutionaries and how they react to what he sees as a predictable, uniform series of opportunities they encounter once a revolution begins. And in each case, the outcome is the same: it is the moderate revolutionaries (the rational opportunists here) who eventually prevail.

Barrington Moore, by contrast, sought to explain the variation in the outcomes of revolutions: why some revolutions led to democracy, others to conservative reaction/fascism, and still others to communism. Had he used the murder metaphor, Moore's answer to this question would be that it all depends on who is the murderer.

There are three traditional farms (countries), all of which are beginning the process of mechanization (economic modernization). All three are owned and operated by tyrannical but relatively uneducated patriarchs (monarchs). Each of these patriarchs has two sons and employs a number of farmhands. Traditionally, it is the elder son (the aristocracy) who inherits, and thus the younger son (the rising bourgeoisie) can expect to receive nothing when the patriarch dies no matter how much effort he devotes to the farm.

On the first farm, the younger son (the bourgeoisie) is energetic and capable, while the elder son (the aristocracy) is not. Increasingly frustrated with life under his father's rule and the expectation of little better when his elder brother takes over, the younger son kills both his father and his brother, takes over the farm, and manages it highly successfully in his preferred mode (democratic capitalism).

What happens on the first farm has a profound effect on the second and third farms. The fathers and the elder sons take strenuous efforts to make sure that the younger sons on these two farms do not do to them what the younger son did to their counterparts on the first farm. It turns out that the younger sons on the second and third farms aren't all that energetic anyway. The elder son on the second farm, though, is. Fearing that his younger brother will eventually become more capable, the elder son kills his father, puts his younger brother under close watch, proceeds to rapidly modernize the farm, and maintains the principle of primogeniture (conservative reaction).

After what happened on both the first and second farms, the father on the third fears both his elder and his younger sons. He then keeps both under close watch, seeing any sign of initiative from either as a negative omen. Neither of these sons is particularly energetic anyway. Conditions on the farm steadily deteriorate. Eventually, it is the farmhands (the peasants) who rise up, kill the father and both sons, and take over the farm for themselves (communism).

Whatever its outcome, Moore saw the opportunity for revolution in all the cases he examined as the inability of traditional governments to effectively modernize their countries. In each case, the motive of the strongest class (bourgeoisie, aristocracy, or peasantry) was not only to overthrow the ancien régime, but to create a nouveau régime through which it could dominate the nation through suppressing (if not eliminating) the other two classes. In addition, the type of revolution that occurs in earlier cases affects and changes the type of revolution that occurs in later cases, which in turn affects and changes the type of revolution that occurs in still later cases.

Ted Robert Gurr's theory of revolution focuses on one factor: motive. Gurr sought to explain why revolution occurred not in the poorest nations, but in those undergoing modernization where significant economic development has already occurred. According to Gurr, the citizens of the former have extremely low expectations of their government and thus do not seek to overthrow it. The expectations of citizens in the latter, by contrast, grow faster than the government can satisfy them, creating a sense of relative deprivation that can lead to revolution.

Gurr's theory can also be illustrated via the murder metaphor. In this case, there are two very poor households, both headed by relatively authoritarian personalities in their forties who are in good health. In both, the adult children are, like the parents (who married quite young), relatively uneducated. They work at low-paying jobs—and contribute a substantial portion of their incomes to the parents. They do not question this arrangement: this is what the parents had to do when they were young adults, and those who are currently young adults expect to receive this sort of support from their children in the future.

In the first household, there is no major change. It never occurs to any of the children that they would be better off without their parents. In the second household, however, the parents win the lottery or receive some other financial windfall. The adult children see this money as an opportunity to pay for college and hence improve their lives dramatically. The parents, though, have other ideas: they want to use the money for buying more lottery tickets, investing in a dubious business investment that one of their "friends" proposes, going on vacation, and other unproductive expenditures. Further, being authoritarian, they expect their adult children to continue to turn over most of their wages to them. As the parents are still relatively young and vigorous, their children—realizing how the windfall could benefit them—quickly acquire a very strong motive to murder their parents before the latter can spend it all. The children, of course, would not have acquired this motive if the parents had not received the windfall.

For Gurr, the coming into being of the motive for revolution (murder) will not necessarily lead to its occurrence. If the government successfully democratizes (if the parents share the wealth), harmony can be restored and revolution (murder) need not occur. But if democratization does not occur (if the parents don't share the wealth), then revolution (murder) is highly likely. Gurr does not focus so much on the opportunity factor. His theory indicates that whoever feels the motive for revolution (murder) intensely will take advantage of, or even create, the opportunity to perpetrate it.

Theda Skocpol criticized Gurr's theory of revolution for focusing on the motive for it, since this was something she saw as always being present: "What society . . . lacks widespread relative deprivation of one sort or another?" (1979, 34). By contrast, her theory of revolution focused on opportunity. For Skocpol, the opportunity for revolution arose as a result of state breakdown, which occurred only in very specific circumstances. Skocpol drew a distinction between the ruling class and the state. While those governing the state were drawn from the ruling class, the interests of the ruling class and the state were not always the same. It was when their interests diverged sharply that state breakdown occurred, thus allowing the oppressed classes to rise up and overthrow them.

Let us return to the household that won the lottery discussed under Gurr. While Skocpol saw the adult children possessing the motive to murder their parents, she saw them as being unable to act on this motive if the parents were of the same mind. The opportunity for murder (revolution) would arise, however, if the parents became seriously divided. If we (arbitrarily) designate the father as the state and the mother as the ruling class, sharp disagreement between the two over, say, how to spend the money from their windfall, would give the adult children the opportunity to play the two parents off against each other, kill the father—perhaps even with the mother's connivance—and then marginalize the mother (whose health has seriously deteriorated as a result of this crisis) afterward. For Skocpol, this scenario need not occur just in the household that received the windfall; it could occur in the one that did not if the parents there also became seriously divided.

In Jack Goldstone's theory of revolution (1991), the opportunity for revolution (in the early modern era) was created by an exogenous variable—rapid population growth. The motive for revolution arose if the ancien régime was unable to raise sufficient revenue to cover the rapidly rising expenses it had to make on this growing population (especially the growing elite population). By contrast, during periods when population growth was low, the ancien régime was able manage its expenses and receipts more successfully, and so maintain stability.

Goldstone's theory can also be illustrated with the murder metaphor. In this case, there is a business owned and managed by a large extended family. The older generation that built up the firm had many children. As these come of age, they all demand positions in the firm. The problem is that the business is not profitable enough to employ all of the members of this large younger generation at the high salaries they expect. While the senior partners all recognize this problem, each of them is determined to bring his own children into the firm. But the more each of them succeeds in doing this, the less profitable the firm becomes. And the less profitable it becomes, the more the head of the firm is blamed for this situation by others in the firm.

In Goldstone's model, however, it is not just the head of the firm whom others in it want to get rid of. In fact, virtually everyone has an incentive to murder everyone else. There is generational conflict between the senior partners and the junior ones who want to replace them. And there is also conflict within each generation, especially the large junior generation vying for position and promotion. As this situation worsens, everyone pursues his or her own individual interest at the expense of the firm's as a whole, which as a result is becoming less competitive than other firms (other countries). If the senior partners can somehow manage to increase revenue, catastrophe can be avoided. But if not, a more vigorous segment of the junior generation may kill off the senior partners (a necessary move since they won't surrender ownership voluntarily) and devise a bolder business plan that can fully absorb the large number of junior partners.

If this junior, or second, generation of partners has few children (for whatever reason), these pressures will not arise as they come of age. This relatively small third generation will easily be absorbed into the firm and will rise up rapidly within it as the second generation retires. But if the third generation has many offspring, the large fourth generation will create problems for the third generation similar to those that the second generation created for the first.

In Goldstone's model, then, high population growth created the opportunity for revolution in the early modern era, but did not make it inevitable. If the ancien régime could successfully manage the financial stresses caused by this growing population, it could avoid revolution. But if it could not manage them (and it sometimes could not), revolution would result.

It would be possible, of course, to depict many other (maybe all other) theories of revolution as variations of the murder metaphor. Just the ones depicted this way here, however, illustrate the point that revolution—like murder—can occur as well as be envisioned in many different ways.

The murder metaphor, however, can also be useful in assessing the question of which theory of revolution is the best, the most accurate, or the most valid. Those who advance such theories are, not surprisingly, quick to point out the weaknesses of other theories and the strengths of their own. And while many theorists—especially those basing theirs on the comparison of relatively few cases—usually state in the beginning of their books that their theory only applies to the cases they examine, by the end of their books and in subsequent works they appear to convince themselves that theirs is the omnipotent general theory that explains all revolution. And when they encounter a case that their theory clearly does not explain, they usually declare that the case is somehow not really an example of revolution.

With regard to murder, however, it is evident that this is so varied a phenomenon that it would be impossible to satisfactorily explain it with a single theory. For to be applicable in all cases, such a theory would have to be so general that it would have little explanatory value. And what is true for understanding murder is also true for understanding revolution: it is simply too varied a phenomenon to be explained by one general theory. Theories that claim to explain revolution in general usually only succeed, at best, in explaining one type or aspect of revolution. This, of course, is extremely useful, and may even be all that is possible. Clearly, though, other types and aspects of revolution need theories to explain them instead of denials of their existence. And since revolution, like murder, is such a highly varied phenomenon, there are many different aspects of it to explain.

In the chapters that follow, I explore some of the aspects of revolution that I think are particularly salient for understanding this phenomenon in the post–Cold War era. Except for chapter 5, each chapter bases its discussion on the work of one particular scholar who previously examined the subject being considered. Chapter 5, by contrast, examines a debate between two scholars. The method of investigation I will use in this study is similar to that employed by Leonard Binder on a related but more regionally circumscribed topic in his *Islamic Liberalism: A Critique of Development Ideologies* (1988). Essentially, this is the method of traditional literary criticism applied to those scholars' works that I am investigating.

Why, then, select certain authors and not others? As Binder acknowledged with regard to his book, "Other works and other writers might have been chosen, and the results would inevitably have been somewhat different" (1988, 21). Ultimately, the justification for selecting the writers I have decided to focus on is the same as Binder made for his selection: "The choice of these authors followed the sequence with which certain theoretical questions arose in my mind, and the authors chosen appeared to me to be the right ones for dealing with the question at hand" (1988, 21). The works of many other scholars, though, will be discussed throughout the book.

The book is divided into three parts, each of which contains two chapters. Part I examines the relationship between class and revolution.

Chapter 1 examines the idea that class conflict is the cause of revolution. This chapter begins with a discussion of one of the most prominent modern theories that saw class conflict as the basis of revolution: Barrington Moore's *Social Origins of Dictatorship and Democracy* (1966). I analyze how the collapse of communism and other events since the publication of his book indicate that Moore's theory needs to be modified with regard to (1) the diffusion and limitation of types of revolution; (2) class conflict and revolution; and (3) nonclass factors and revolution. Moore theorized that the success of one type of revolution in a few countries at one time would serve to prevent its later occurrence in other countries. This view, however, now appears to be mistaken, especially with regard to the spread of democratic capitalism. Regarding class conflict, Moore assumed that patterns of class dominance established by a revolution remained permanently frozen afterward. But as the experience of several states in the twentieth century has shown, social classes and relations among them can undergo considerable evolution after a revolution. And while Moore paid little attention to the role played by religious and nationalist conflict in revolution, such divisions appear to be the most salient feature of several ongoing attempts at revolution.

Chapter 2 focuses on social evolution in societies that have experienced revolution. In it, I argue that the theory of revolution advanced by the Moroccan scholar Abdallah Laroui in the 1960s and 1970s is especially useful for understanding the evolution of revolutionary regimes. Unlike classic Marxism and the many "Marxian" interpretations of revolution drawing inspiration from it, Laroui's theory of revolution provides an explanation of how the embrace of capitalism and the West by revolutionary regimes is, far from being aberrant behavior, the logical consequence of the normal process of embourgeoisement in revolutionary states. Indeed, the fact that most revolutionary regimes have embraced embourgeoisement in recent years while only a handful have failed to do so indicates that the latter are somehow abnormal cases.

Part II examines the relationship between nationalism and revolution.

Chapter 3 extends to revolution the concept of *ressentiment,* which Liah Greenfeld applied to nationalism. Ressentiment arises from the perception that one's own nation is "falling behind" others along with the desire to "rectify" this situation. Those who make revolution do not just have domestic ambitions, but international ones as well. In addition to overthrowing the existing regime and replacing it with another, revolutionaries have sought to enhance the status of their country internationally. The minimum international goal of anticolonial "nationalist" revolutionaries has been to expel foreign rule from their country and establish independent statehood. The maximum goal of revolutionaries has been to establish, or reestablish, their nation as a great power. This chapter examines how successful revolutionaries and revolutionary regimes have been at achieving their ressentiment-based international goals, as well as how their sense of ressentiment tends to evolve over time.

Chapter 4 discusses how nationalist revolution remains a prominent feature of the post–Cold War era in the form of the many "secessionist" struggles that began during the Cold War era (or even earlier) and the many new such conflicts that the end of the Cold War appears to have helped ignite. I examine how secessionist efforts can be understood as a form of nationalist revolution arising from causes similar to what Ted Robert Gurr argued was an important cause of revolution in general: relative deprivation. But while Gurr emphasized the economic aspect of relative deprivation as a cause of revolution, I argue here that secessionist revolution results more from a sense of political relative deprivation, and that this sense of political relative deprivation has become especially heightened in the post–Cold War era.

Part III examines the relationship between democracy and revolution.

Chapter 5 examines the debate between Jeff Goodwin and Eric Selbin about whether or not the "age of revolution" is over. While the future of revolution cannot be definitively foreseen, I seek to show how approaching this question with different assumptions can point to different answers to it. I discuss the implications for the future of revolution initially under the assumption that revolution and democracy are inversely related, and then again after relaxing this assumption. In each case, I examine how assuming that democratization occurs on either a linear basis or a cyclical one affects the analysis. I conclude by observing that the relationship between democracy and revolution is subject to change because these are both continually evolving phenomena.

Chapter 6 discusses the response of democratic status quo powers to revolution through reexamining Jeane Kirkpatrick's advocating that the United States support "good" authoritarian regimes in order to prevent "bad" totalitarian ones from replacing them. While Kirkpatrick justified support for authoritarian regimes on the basis that they could undergo democratization while totalitarian ones could not, events since 1989 have shown that many "totalitarian" regimes have made the transition to democracy more successfully than many "authoritarian" ones. Yet the United States continues to pursue the Kirkpatrick logic in the post–Cold War era, especially in the Muslim world. The ramifications of its doing so are then discussed.

PART I

CLASS AND REVOLUTION

CHAPTER 1

CLASS CONFLICT AND REVOLUTION
Reflections on Barrington Moore

IN LIGHT OF THE COLLAPSE OF COMMUNISM in the former Soviet bloc
and the adoption of capitalism by China, the most important state
that continues to be ruled by a communist party, does it still make
sense to think of class conflict as a cause of revolution?

The collapse of communism, it must be noted, does not invali-
date the notion of class conflict—usually envisioned as the struggle
between a smaller group enjoying significant economic and political power on the one hand and a larger group possessing substantially less of these attributes on the other. Class conflict existed long
before the "proletarian" or "peasant" revolutions of the twentieth
century or even the "bourgeois" revolutions of the seventeenth and
eighteenth centuries. Aristotle, for example, discussed this phenomenon: "[T]he prime division of classes in a state is into the well-
to-do and the propertyless. Further, owing to the fact that the one
class is for the most part numerically small, the other large, these
two appear as antagonistic classes" (1962, 158).[1] Class conflict
was also the predominant theme in Livy's description of the politics
of the Roman Republic (Livy 1960, 1982), as well as Machiavelli's
of republican politics generally (Machiavelli 1970, 115–24).

Class conflict, then, was an important feature of how politics were envisioned long before Marx. It was Marx and his followers, though, who popularized the idea that class conflict should, could, and inevitably would lead to socialist revolution in which the proletariat would triumph over the bourgeoisie (Kolakowski 1978, vol. 1). Inspired by Marx's vision of an international class struggle, Lenin led a victorious revolutionary movement that sought both to build a socialist state in Russia and foster the spread of socialist revolution throughout the rest of the world (Tucker 1975, 542–9). While this latter ambition was not achieved, Marxist movements inspired by Lenin did lead successful revolutions in many different countries in several parts of the world (Katz 1997, 25–40).

Marxists, though, were not the only twentieth-century revolutionaries to conceive of politics in terms of class conflict. In addition to opposing Western imperialism and Zionism, Arab nationalists excoriated the Arab world's monarchies and traditional elites for collaborating with the West. Arab nationalist regimes also claimed to rule on behalf of the "Arab masses" (Nasser 1955; Kerr 1971, 1–7). Similarly, class conflict was a part of the Ayatollah Khomeini's Islamic fundamentalist revolutionary vision, which saw a struggle between a secularized Muslim elite serving the interests of the West on the one hand and the oppressed Muslim masses on the other (Abrahamian 1993, 47–50).

But the events of the late twentieth century—particularly the collapse of communism—indicate that the relationship between class struggle and revolution in the post–Cold War era is no longer what it was popularly thought to be (whether accurately or not) earlier in the century. Because neither class conflict (a phenomenon that has been in existence since long before Aristotle) nor revolution (which is currently ongoing in many countries) seems likely to disappear, understanding how they relate to each other at present is clearly important.

This, of course, is an enormous task. I certainly do not purport to make a definitive statement about the present relationship between class conflict and revolution. What I seek to do instead is to examine how the collapse of communism and subsequent events suggest how one of the most prominent statements about this relationship—Barrington Moore's *Social Origins of Dictatorships and Democracy* (1966)—needs to be modified.

MOORE'S THEORY OF REVOLUTION

What made Moore's theory of revolution noteworthy was that it provided a far more sophisticated analysis of the relationship between class conflict and revolution than did orthodox Marxist theories of revolution (Skocpol 1994, 29–30). Unlike orthodox Marxists, Moore did not describe the proletariat as playing a major role in any of the eight countries that he examined (Britain, France, the United States, Germany, Japan, Russia, China, and India).[2] Indeed, Moore did not appear to see the proletariat as playing any significant role in these revolutions. Although there are long entries for "Bourgeoisie"; "Classes, landed upper"; "Gentry"; and "Peasantry" in his index, there are none for either proletariat or workers. "Laborers" appears as an entry, but as the second part of the entry—"or rural proletariat"—indicates, this does not apply to urban laborers (1966, 547–59). For Moore, then, the three most important classes were the bourgeoisie, the landed aristocracy, and the peasantry.

Using class conflict as the key variable for understanding revolution, Moore sought to explain why capitalist democracy triumphed in Britain, France, and the United States; fascism in Germany and Japan; and communism in Russia and China. According to Moore, capitalist democracy triumphed in Britain, France, and the United States because in these countries the bourgeoisie was relatively strong, the peasantry was weak, and the aristocracy was either becoming embourgeoised itself (Britain), divided between embourgeoised and unembourgeoised elements (France), or nonexistent (the United States). Fascism, though, triumphed in Germany and Japan where the aristocracy was strong, the bourgeoisie was dependent on the aristocracy, and the peasantry was weak. And communism triumphed in Russia and China, where both the bourgeoisie and the aristocracy were weak, and hence unable to control the peasantry when revolution came (1966, xiv-xvi).

Unlike orthodox Marxists, who saw capitalist democratic revolution as setting the stage for later proletarian revolution when the "contradictions" they saw as inherent in capitalism had fully developed, Moore seemed to regard the capitalist democratic revolutions in Britain, France, and the United States on the one hand and the communist revolutions in Russia and China on the other as permanently deciding their respective "routes to modern society." Moore saw the German and Japanese fascism that he claimed was the result of their nineteenth-century conservative "revolutions from above" as coming to an end only through military defeat and foreign occupation, not the actions of internal forces. (Moore insisted that conservative aristocratic revolution and fascism were linked, and that this "route to modernity" was far less stable than the other two.)[3] By contrast, Moore did not anticipate that communism would also prove to be unstable or that it would eventually give rise to capitalism in both Russia and China. Needless to say, he was not alone!

The relative strength of the three most important classes vis-à-vis one another, however, was not the only determinant of what type of revolution succeeded in each particular country. According to Moore, the type of revolution that succeeded in one country affected the type of revolution that could succeed in another:

> To a very limited extent these three types—bourgeois revolutions culminating in the Western form of democracy, conservative revolutions from above ending in fascism, and peasant revolutions leading to communism—may constitute alternative routes and choices. They are much more clearly successive historical stages. As such, they display a limited determinate relation to each other. The methods of modernization chosen in one country change the dimensions of the problem for the next countries who take the step. . . . Without the prior democratic modernization of England, the reactionary methods adopted in Germany and Japan would scarcely have been possible. Without both the capitalist and reactionary experiences, the communist method would have been something entirely different, if it had come into existence at all. (1966, 413–14)

Moore did not really explain why the victory of one type of revolution in some countries during one period would preclude it from occurring in others later. He himself wrote, "It is or should be quite obvious that certain institutional arrangements such as feudalism, absolute monarchy, and capitalism, rise, have their day, and pass away" (1966, 427). Moore apparently regarded this idea as being so self-evident as not to require an elaborate explanation.

This type of reasoning was intellectually popular during the heyday of the dependency theorists in the late 1960s and 1970s. They argued that capitalist economic development in the West was only able to occur as a result of the West exploiting, or underdeveloping, the Third World. The global expansion of the Western capitalist system, they claimed, perpetuated underdevelopment elsewhere, thereby necessitating that the Third World opt out of the Western capitalist system and pursue its own autonomous development instead (Knutsen 1997, 250–1). But in addition to seeing capitalism as a self-limiting phenomenon, Moore saw communism as being one too. Thus, Moore anticipated that if social revolution ever occurred in India (and he saw this as likely), "it will not necessarily take the form of a communist-led peasant revolution." (1966, 482). Indeed, he saw "Indian diffidence" to capitalist democracy, fascism, and communism as being "a negative critical reaction to all three forms of prior historical experience" (1966, 414).[4]

Social Origins had a major impact on the work of subsequent scholars. In the preface to her own *magnum opus* on revolution, Theda Skocpol wrote, "My most fundamental scholarly debt is to Barrington Moore, Jr." (1979, xv). Elsewhere, she described *Social Origins* as "an unparalleled positive contribution to the scientific enterprise of understanding modernization" (1994, 48). Jack Goldstone noted that many of the points developed by later scholars were introduced by Moore (Goldstone 1980, 434). Haim Gerber used Moore's theory as a model for explaining the historical evolution of the modern Middle East (Gerber 1987). Tim McDaniel undertook a modification of Moore's theory in order to compare the Russian and Iranian Revolutions of 1917 and 1979 (McDaniel 1991, 5–11). John Foran described *Social Origins* as having "set the stage for a series of later works" on revolution (1994, 161).[5]

Like other such influential books, *Social Origins* was criticized from many different perspectives in the years just after it was published.[6] These contemporary critiques which, like the book itself, were written in the context of the ongoing Cold War, will not be discussed here. What is to be considered here instead is what subsequent events, particularly the collapse of communism, tell us about how Moore's theory needs to be modified with regard to (1) the diffusion and limitation of types of revolution; (2) class conflict and revolution; and (3) nonclass factors and revolution.

THE DIFFUSION AND LIMITATION OF TYPES OF REVOLUTION

When *Social Origins* was published in 1966, and for two decades afterward, the idea that capitalist democracy had already reached its zenith and was losing ground to the spreading tide of communism was prevalent not just among those sympathetic toward Marxism, but among some of communism's strongest opponents as well (Fukuyama 1992, 7–9).[7] This seemed especially true during the mid and late 1970s when Marxist regimes came to power in so many Third World countries, including South Vietnam, Cambodia, and Laos in Southeast Asia; Ethiopia, Angola, Mozambique, and Guinea-Bissau in Africa; Afghanistan in South Asia; and Grenada and Nicaragua in the Caribbean. Even in the 1980s, strong Marxist insurgencies were being waged in El Salvador, Guatemala, Peru, the Philippines, and elsewhere.

During these years, the spread of capitalist democracy to other countries did not seem like a very serious prospect. Indeed, the prospects for capitalist democracy—or capitalism without democracy—surviving in just those countries where it already existed seemed to be far more in question. Thus, Moore's contention that the democratic capitalism that had arisen in a few countries during the seventeenth, eighteenth, and nineteenth centuries had become "hopelessly anachronistic" by the latter half of the twentieth century did not seem unreasonable to many, especially in the 1970s and early 1980s.

In retrospect, of course, it is not democratic capitalism that appears to be anachronistic, but Moore's statement about it being so. Since the publication of *Social Origins*, democracy has spread to several states that only possessed capitalism (in Southern Europe in the 1970s, Latin America and Asia in the 1980s, and Africa—

particularly South Africa—in the 1990s), and democratic capitalism to several states that possessed neither (in Eastern Europe in 1989 and the former Soviet Union in 1991). While the universal spread of democratic capitalism predicted by Francis Fukuyama (1992) does not appear to be imminent, nothing about its existence in some countries appears to prevent its spread to others. The obstacles to its spread to those countries where it has not yet done so appear to be primarily internal ones.

A similar argument could have been made about communism in the 1970s. The success of Marxist revolution in Russia in 1917 and China in 1949 did not, as Moore implied, prevent the spread of Marxist revolution to many Third World countries, especially in the 1970s. Nor did the original fascist revolution in Italy prevent the coming to power of regimes espousing similar ideologies in Germany, Austria, Hungary, Romania, Spain, and Portugal in Europe.

It does not seem, then, that the occurrence of one type of revolution in two or three "great power" countries prevents a similar type of revolution from occurring elsewhere in other countries— even much later. If anything, the opposite appears to be true: the occurrence of a particular type of revolution in even one "great power" country can facilitate the spread of a similar form of government and socioeconomic system to other countries via revolution or some other means. It is doubtful, for example, whether fascist revolution would have triumphed in Spain without assistance from Germany and Italy. It is even more doubtful that Marxism would have spread to Eastern Europe had it not been imposed "from without" by the Soviet Union. Soviet assistance also played a role in the spread of Marxist revolution to the Third World, though the extent to which the Russian, Chinese, North Vietnamese, and Cuban Revolutions inspired emulation should not be underestimated.[8] Similarly, the United States and Western Europe played a role in the many democratic transformations that took place from the 1970s to the 1990s, both through some form of involvement in them and serving as a model for those seeking to end dictatorships.[9]

Instead of the success of one type of revolution precluding similar ones later, it is the defeat or failure of one of the originals of a type of revolution that seems far more likely to do this. There have, for example, been no fascist revolutions after the defeat of the Axis powers in 1945. After the defeat of Arab nationalist Egypt and Syria by Israel in 1967, two Arab nationalist revolutions (really just coups d'état) did occur in Libya and Sudan in 1969. But not only have there been no further such revolutions since then, but the existing Arab nationalist regimes have become vulnerable to Islamic fundamentalist revolutionaries.[10] It would appear that there is virtually no prospect for the success of communist revolution anywhere in the wake of the double collapse of communism and of the USSR. The Marxist revolutionary movement, which was still active in many Third World countries through the late 1980s, virtually collapsed in the early 1990s (Katz 1997, 83–107).

But while, contrary to Moore's theory, successful revolution in one country is more likely to facilitate than preclude similar revolutions elsewhere, whether or not it actually does is greatly affected by the internal situation in other countries. And as Moore demonstrated just with the cases he examined, this can vary greatly with respect to the relative strength of different social classes vis-à-vis one another. This leads us, then, to a discussion of class conflict and revolution from a post–Cold War perspective.

CLASS CONFLICT AND REVOLUTION

In theories that regard class conflict as the basis for revolution, the boundaries between classes are usually portrayed as being sharp and clear. Moore's conception of social class was not as rigid as that of orthodox Marxists, but the presumption of basically conflictual relations among relatively cohesive social classes lay at the heart of Moore's theory of revolution.

Social classes, of course, are not always cohesive, since people do not always act in accordance with the "class interests" that theorists ascribe to them. The classic example of this was the pre-revolutionary Russian Marxists, many of whom—including Lenin—were children of the privileged classes (McCauley 1993, 9; Figes 1996, 141–5). Many other successful twentieth-century revolutionary movements that claimed to act on behalf of the proletariat and the peasantry were also led by people who came from neither (Wickham-Crowley 1992, 23–5; Colburn 1994, 44).

It is not just revolutionary leaders, however, that do not necessarily pursue their ascribed class interests, but much larger groups as well. Goldstone, for example, has shown that the French Revolution was not simply a struggle between the bourgeoisie and the aristocracy as it has often been described—including by Moore. Instead, he saw it partly as a conflict between the more economically successful segments of both the bourgeoisie and aristocracy on the one hand and the less successful segments of each on the other (1991, 243–7). In her comparative study of the Iranian and Nicaraguan cases, Farideh Farhi observed that these revolutions were not the work of any single class, but of a multiclass alliance against the state (1990, 18).

These examples point to another problem with Moore's theory of the relationship between class conflict and revolution: as in Machiavelli's description of the complex class relations of the past, social classes can be in conflict but they may also cooperate with one another. Indeed, their relations may involve both conflict and cooperation simultaneously.

To the extent that multiclass alliances occur in them, revolutions can be seen more as acts of class cooperation than class conflict. Nor should this be surprising: given the difficulties in effecting a revolution, they are likely to be more readily overcome by an alliance of classes than by one acting exclusively by and for itself. Instances of the leadership of revolutionary movements that claimed to fight on behalf of the workers and peasants actually coming from more privileged class backgrounds are examples of multiclass alliances being present. Even orthodox Marxist-Leninists recognized the desirability of a "united front" drawn from different social groups against a common enemy.[11]

Yet another problem with Moore's theory of the relationship between class conflict and revolution is its relatively static conception of social classes over time. Moore saw revolution as arising through the process of economic modernization which, among other effects, both weakened traditional autocratic governments and intensified class conflict. Once the traditional autocratic government was overthrown, the strongest (or least weak) of the three most important social classes (bourgeoisie, aristocracy, and peasantry for Moore) would then succeed to power and impose its politico-economic preferences on the nation as a whole. And in Moore's theory, whichever class was victorious in the revolution would then dominate the nation permanently—except, as in the case of fascist Germany and Japan, where the predominant class emerging from the revolution was defeated by external powers.

For Moore, in other words, the pattern of class dominance established in a country by a revolution remained inert afterward, at least as far as internal evolution was concerned. But as the experience of several states in the twentieth century indicates, social classes and relations among them can undergo considerable evolution after a revolution. Stalin in Russia and Mao in China engineered the forced conversion of a substantial proportion of the peasantry into an urban proletariat. More recently, both countries have experienced the rapid growth of an indigenous bourgeoisie drawn from, among other sources, the ranks of communist party bureaucrats and economic managers. Previous claims to being the representatives of the workers and peasants clearly did not prevent these people from redefining their own class interests.

This process of social class evolution, of course, is not just present in postrevolutionary states, but more generally throughout the world. Virtually all countries have experienced, or are experiencing, the migration of peasants from rural to urban areas where they, sooner or later, undergo proletarianization, embourgeoisement, or some other "modernizing" transformation. If not dispossessed through revolution, as in some of Moore's cases, the traditional aristocracy has been increasingly beset by the exigencies of the market. In the face of this all-pervasive challenge, individual aristocrats have either adjusted to market forces and become embourgeoised, or failed to do so and become impoverished. While bourgeoisies are being reconstructed many years or even decades after the victory of Marxist revolution destroyed them in many countries, the aristocracy has not regained lost ground anywhere. Although it played a large role in Moore's theory of revolution, the aristocracy now seems to be disappearing even faster than the peasantry.

This has obvious implications for the future of revolution. To the extent that peasantries are diminishing and aristocracies are disappearing, peasant and especially aristocratic revolutions are becoming less and less likely. If peasants who move to the cities mainly become workers, this would suggest that the prospects for proletarian revolution should increase. But, as was argued earlier, the collapse of communism does not appear likely to enhance the popularity of proletarian revolution—especially at a time when it is becoming easier for intelligent, ambitious workers to join the ranks of the bourgeoisie.

While Moore saw the bourgeoisie as becoming increasingly archaic over time, it is the one class that in fact seems to be growing larger through members of other social classes voluntarily—even enthusiastically—joining it. This increasing strength of the bourgeoisie compared to other classes implies that where capitalist democracy does not yet exist, the most likely future type of revolution is the capitalist democratic variety. And where capitalist democracy does exist, it appears unlikely that class-based revolution can succeed or even occur as nonbourgeois classes increasingly merge with the bourgeoisie. Nor does the bourgeoisie seem likely to launch a revolution when it already controls a capitalist democratic state. If not the end of history, then, the rise of the bourgeoisie and capitalist democracy appear to lead toward the end of revolution.

NONCLASS FACTORS AND REVOLUTION

This happy prospect, however, will not necessarily occur—and this is due to an even more fundamental problem with Moore's theory of revolution as well as other class-based ones: class conflict is not the only possible cause of revolution. Revolution can also be the result of ethnic or religious conflict.

A nationalist factor served to enhance the appeal of Marxist revolutionary movements across class lines in several cases, including China, where the Marxists gained and the Nationalists lost prestige for their respective resistance efforts against the Japanese invaders (Lomperis 1996, 140–44); Vietnam, where the Marxists fought first against French colonialists and then American interventionists (Lomperis 1996, 92–104), and South Yemen, where the Marxist opposition fought against the British, the hereditary sultans whom the British hoped to grant independence to, and a Nasserist opposition movement dependent on Egypt (Halliday 1974, 190–1). Similarly, the Islamic revolutionaries of Iran were able to rally the support of many segments of Iranian society against a ruler widely seen as being the puppet of the United States (Foran 1994, 178–81).

There clearly existed a "haves vs. have-nots" element in all these revolutionary struggles. But the nationalist struggle against foreign rule or intervention was also a salient factor. Weak support for non-Marxist governments or alternative opposition groups in these cases seems to have been due more to their compromising links to foreign powers than to any enduring class-based opposition to capitalism per se.[12]

A significant ethnic or religious division also exists in many of the ongoing revolutionary struggles in the post–Cold War era. The Zapatistas and the Popular Revolutionary Army in southern Mexico and what remains of Sendero Luminoso in Peru are both predominantly native American groups fighting European- or mestizo-dominated governments. Al-Jama 'a al-Islamiyya in Egypt is drawn predominantly from the traditionally dispossessed southerners opposed to the northern-dominated government and the northern-dominated Islamic opposition movements (Fandy 1994). Other examples include Hamas in the West Bank (Palestinians opposed to Israeli occupation), the Kurds in eastern Turkey and northern Iraq, the Shi'ites in southern Iraq (resisting Saddam Hussein's Sunni minority regime), the Kashmiris in India (a predominantly Muslim region seeking secession from Hindu-dominated India), the Tamil Tigers in Sri Lanka (fighting against a Sinhalese-dominated government), the Uighurs and Tibetans in China, and until recently (it seems), the Irish Republican Army in Northern Ireland (Irish Catholic Nationalists fighting against Irish Protestant Unionists).

Moore himself seemed to acknowledge the importance of the ethnic factor in his vision of the future when he predicted that revolution in India "will not necessarily take the form of a communist-led peasant revolution. A turn to the right or fragmentation along regional lines, or some combination of these two, seems much more probable in the light of India's social structure" (1966, 482). Since Moore wrote this, both of these tendencies have gained strength in India. "Fragmentation along regional lines" is obviously based on religion and/or ethnicity, as is the "turn to the right," in the form of rising Hindu fundamentalism (Juergensmeyer 1993, 78–99).

Like class boundaries, ethnic boundaries do not necessarily remain fixed. Sociologist J. Milton Yinger has described how ethnic distinctions can diminish over time (1994, 1–166). And even where ethnic and religious boundaries do remain relatively firm, they need not coincide with class boundaries. But where they do coincide, it is the existence of firm ethnic and religious boundaries that may be the principle obstacle to the disappearance of class boundaries in general and to the embourgeoisement of hitherto deprived ethnic and religious groups in particular. It is where ethnic and religious barriers serve to prevent such groups from experiencing embourgeoisement that, in so many cases, they seek to improve their overall status through revolution.

CHAPTER 2

THE EMBOURGEOISEMENT OF REVOLUTIONARY REGIMES

Reflections on Abdallah Laroui

WITH THE DOWNFALL OF ALMOST ALL communist governments and the wholehearted adoption of capitalism by most of the few remaining ones, Marxist class analysis and theories of revolution have, to put it mildly, fallen into disfavor. Few now predict that the proletariat or the peasantry will anywhere rise up to overthrow the bourgeoisie and establish socialism. And those who do predict this are not taken seriously.

Revolutionaries, however, are active in many countries. Some, such as the Zapatistas in Mexico as well as Sendero Luminoso and Tupac Amaru in Peru, are Marxists of one variety or another. These groups, though, appear to have little prospect of leading a successful revolution, and no prospect of "building socialism" even if they do (Palmer 1996; Dresser 1997). By contrast, religious fundamentalist revolutionary groups are active in many countries and appear to enjoy much greater prospects for leading successful revolutions than do the few remaining Marxist revolutionary groups (Juergensmeyer 1993). This is especially true in the Muslim world, where Islamic revolutionary groups have already come to power in three countries (Iran, Sudan, and Afghanistan), and are actively attempting to do so in many others (Roy 1994).

In classic Marxism, feudalism is replaced by capitalism, which is in turn replaced by socialism. But the Islamic revolution in Iran defied Soviet observers as it appeared to be neither capitalist nor socialist (Papp 1985, 59–61). Nor, obviously, did classic Marxism predict the downfall of socialism and its replacement by capitalism in the late twentieth century.

Yet virtually all the revolutions of the twentieth century— Marxist-Leninist, Arab nationalist, Islamic fundamentalist, or other religious and/or nationalist varieties—had or have a highly important class element. These were all conflicts in which the struggle between the "haves" and the "have-nots" played an important role. A theory of revolution needs to account for the class factor in order to understand this phenomenon fully, even after the downfall of communism.

It will be argued here that the theory of revolution advanced by the Moroccan scholar Abdallah Laroui in the 1960s and 1970s is especially useful for understanding revolution in the post–Cold War era. Unlike classic Marxism and the many "Marxian" interpretations of revolution drawing inspiration from it, Laroui's theory of revolution provides an explanation of how the embrace of capitalism and the West by revolutionary regimes, far from being aberrant behavior, is the logical consequence of the normal process of embourgeoisement in revolutionary states.

In this chapter, I will (1) examine the inadequacy of Marxist and "Marxian" theories in explaining the evolution of revolutionary regimes occurring in recent years; (2) outline Laroui's theory of revolution and discuss how it differs from Marxist and "Marxian" theories; (3) analyze the extent to which Laroui's vision appears applicable at present; and (4) discuss the implications of Laroui's theory for the future.

MARXIST AND "MARXIAN" THEORIES

During the nineteenth and twentieth centuries, there have been a wide variety of viewpoints held by, and disputation among, thinkers who considered themselves to be Marxist. Marxist thinking, then, was not a uniform phenomenon, and portraying it as such must be avoided. Nevertheless, Marxist thinkers as a whole shared certain basic assumptions about history and what its direction was. For Marxists, the nineteenth and twentieth centuries was the era in which the main focus of history was the struggle between the bourgeoisie on the one hand and the proletariat and/or the peasantry on the other—the struggle between capitalism and socialism. Marxists also believed that they knew the outcome of this struggle: capitalism would inevitably lose out to socialism, which would then reign triumphant.[1]

There was a great divide in the Marxist tradition between those who believed that the triumph of socialism could occur peacefully and democratically (the social-democratic tradition) and those who believed it could only occur through violent revolution (the communist tradition). Among the latter, there were differences over the precise means by which they envisioned revolution occurring. But in whatever manner it occurred, all believed that socialism was the "end of history." And once the revolution succeeded, the worker and/or peasant solidarity that was one of the most important ingredients of that success would remain strong as it faced the task of "building socialism."

Socialist revolutionary regimes would, of course, be threatened by the capitalist imperialists externally and "class enemies" internally; this was a basic tenet of Marxism-Leninism. Marxist-Leninists, however, did not expect that the workers and peasants in whose name the revolution had been made would seek to dismantle socialism (anyone who sought this was, by definition, not a worker or peasant). Even less did they expect that Marxist-Leninist ruling parties would seek to dismantle socialism or their own monopoly on power.

Throughout much of the twentieth century, Marxist-Leninists seemed to believe that the most likely way in which a revolutionary socialist government could be overthrown was through a successful "imperialist" invasion. However, the deployment of a powerful nuclear arsenal by the USSR from 1949 on made such an invasion increasingly risky for the "imperialists," and hence unlikely. The frustration of the American effort to halt the spread of Marxist revolution in Indochina and the development of the "Vietnam syndrome" made "imperialist" invasion against aspiring Marxist revolutionaries, much less an established Marxist-Leninist regime, even less likely. By 1980, Moscow appeared to be calling for an extension of the Brezhnev Doctrine (the justification for the Soviet use of force to prevent the downfall of communist regimes in Eastern Europe) to Third World Marxist states (Katz 1982, 114–15).

Marxists, of course, were not the only ones to write about revolution. Theories of revolution—often more sophisticated than Marxist-Leninist ones—were advanced by several non-Marxist Western scholars such as Barrington Moore (1966) and Theda Skocpol (1979). Ironically, while these non-Marxist as well as anti-Marxist thinkers often took issue with it, they usually accepted key elements of Marxism-Leninism with regard to revolution. Leftist but non-Marxist scholars seemed to agree (though for different reasons) with Marxist-Leninist predictions about socialist revolution being inevitable, at least in the Third World. Nor did they challenge the notion that such revolutions were irreversible. Anti-Marxist theorists tended to see such revolutions as not necessarily inevitable, but definitely irreversible once they occurred (Kirkpatrick 1979; Wiles 1985).

To the extent, then, that non-Marxist and even anti-Marxist thinkers and policymakers accepted certain Marxist or Marxist-Leninist assumptions about revolution, they can be described as "Marxian." And like their Marxist brethren, these "Marxian" theorists did not predict the downfall of communism, or explain it after the fact.

LAROUI'S THEORY OF REVOLUTION

Abdallah Laroui did not set out to write a general theory of revolution, but sought instead to explain why Arab nationalist revolutions occurred and how Arab nationalist regimes evolved after coming to power. He published two books on this subject: *L'idéologie arabe contemporaine* (1967), and *The Crisis of the Arab Intellectual: Traditionalism or Historicism?* (1976).

In these books, Laroui could be seen as someone attempting to apply Marxist analysis to the Arab world. Laroui made frequent reference to Marx and accepted Marx's notion that class struggle was the predominant feature of politics. However, he felt that Marx, and Western Marxist analysis generally, did not accurately describe the nature of class conflict in the Arab states of the mid-twentieth century before the success of Arab nationalist revolution. Like the Marxists, Laroui saw the bourgeoisie as one of the two principle protagonists in the class struggle. Unlike the Marxists, however, he saw both the proletariat and the peasantry as being too weak to challenge the bourgeoisie. In the Arab states, however, there was another class that was strong enough to do so: the petite bourgeoisie (1976, 162–3).

In Laroui's terms, the Arab petite bourgeoisie has the following characteristics:

- It represents the majority of the urban population, so that town life is synonymous with petit-bourgeois life, above all when the economically or politically dominant class is a foreign one.
- It indeed represents a minority in relation to the mass of peasants; but these, insofar as they leave the communal framework to enter a cash economy, transform themselves into small independent landholders before social differentiation reinforces the large and middling properties and increases the number of agricultural workers and landless peasants; they consolidate the power of the urban petite bourgeoisie since both classes share an attachment to independence and to private property (1976, 163).

Unlike the glowing terms in which most Marxists (or the hysterical terms in which most anti-Marxists) described how the revolutionary proletariat and/or peasantry sought to "build socialism," Laroui portrayed the "revolutionary" petite bourgeoisie as possessing a

mundane "attachment to . . . private property." Indeed, he characterized the petite bourgeoisie as seeking immediate access to the
high-consumption lifestyle that it sees the bourgeoisie enjoying.
In its consumerist aspirations, the Arab petite bourgeoisie is
"modern"—even "Western." On the other hand, it is also extremely traditional. It fears that Westernization will destroy Arab
culture and identity, and thus seeks to halt the Arab bourgeoisie's
seeming collaboration in this process by isolating the Arab world
from the West through the assertion of an anti-Western Arab nationalism. There is an inherent duality, then, in how the Arab petite bourgeoisie views the West: it seeks to emulate the West in
some ways, but also rejects it. Laroui "argues that it is the culture
of this class, rather than anything inherently Islamic or Arab,
which leads to the rejection of the dialogue with the West" (Binder
1988, 337).

In class terms, Laroui saw Arab nationalist revolution as the
overthrow of the bourgeoisie by the petite bourgeoisie. The petite
bourgeoisie's success was due largely to the small size and relative
weakness of the bourgeoisie at the time of its overthrow. In Laroui's
theory, then, 'Abd al-Nasir's "petit bourgeois Egyptian state represents not a transition to bourgeois domination, but a premature
overthrow of the bourgeois state in Egypt. It was premature because
the process of embourgeoisement . . . had not yet been achieved
when the bourgeois state of pre-1952 Egypt was overthrown"
(Binder 1988, 332).

But in addition to examining what led up to Arab nationalist
revolution, Laroui also theorized about what happened afterward.
While Arab nationalist revolution brought the petite bourgeoisie to
power, the new regime did not represent that class as a whole. It was
only a small part of the petite bourgeoisie that ruled over the rest of
the nation, including the rest of the petite bourgeoisie.

The Arab nationalist regimes that arose in the 1950s and 1960s
had many ambitions: to bring about "revolutionary socialism," to
"stand up to" Israel and its Western backers, to overthrow "back-
ward" Arab monarchies, and most ambitiously, to unite the Arab
world into one great state (Nasser 1955; Kerr 1971, 1–7). But the
petit bourgeois Arab nationalist regime placed the highest priority

on one goal: remaining in power. All other ambitions were subordinate to this overriding ambition, and indeed, were only pursued insofar as the regime believed (sometimes mistakenly) they supported it. And the petit bourgeois regime sought to take full advantage of modern technology (such as sophisticated weapons) in order to remain in power (Laroui 1976, 165–6).

To do this, the petit bourgeois regime seeks to promote modernization and traditionalism simultaneously: "On the one hand it profits from modern culture . . . by economically and militarily consolidating its power; on the other hand it profits from its fidelity to traditional culture by legitimizing an exclusive authority" (Laroui 1976, 163–4). The authoritarian aspects of traditional culture, then, are utilized by the regime to justify not allowing the political modernization or Westernization that could lead to its authority being challenged.

The regime's desire to foster some aspects of modernization while retaining some aspects of traditionalism required a dualistic educational policy:

> The scientific, technological, commercial, and other institutes, which prepare students for service in the modern sector, offer (frequently in a foreign language) the most advanced programs and methods. Thus is educated, on a pattern different from that of the nation at large, a bureaucratic elite that is detached from the population and committed to the service of the State. . . . As for the other educational institutes . . . either they remain faithful to the traditional methods or they are dedicated to defending the same values in a slightly updated manner (Laroui 1976, 165).

What happens, though, is that the bureaucratic elite that receives a modern higher education gradually changes its mind about some of the most firmly held beliefs and policies of the petit bourgeois regime when it first came to power. For example, while the original petit bourgeois leadership saw nationalization as an economic panacea, the bureaucratic elite increasingly comes to see the disadvantages of a state-run economy and the advantages of free enterprise. While the initial revolutionary leadership seemed to delight in "confronting" the West when it first came to power, the bureaucratic elite it raises up finds this counterproductive to cooperation with the West, which it values more and more.

In short, while it might not necessarily value democracy, the educated bureaucratic elite does become embourgeoised. Its plan of action increasingly becomes the embourgeoisement of society as a whole—a task that the prerevolutionary bourgeoisie signally failed to accomplish before it was overthrown.

And as far as Laroui is concerned, this is a highly positive development. For, as Binder put it, Laroui "believes that the establishment of a bourgeois state is a prerequisite to the achievement of an Islamic-Arab cultural authenticity, which can then enter into a conversation with the West on the basis of cultural equality" (1988, 338). The tragedy of Arab nationalist revolution is that it unnecessarily delays this realization: "Laroui seems to think that a traditional monarch can do a better job of completing the 'bourgeois revolution' and constructing a bourgeois state than can a Bonapartist ruler such as Nasser" (Binder 1988, 337). This, of course, is a highly prudent point of view for a scholar making his career in the Kingdom of Morocco to espouse, but if embourgeoisement is the eventual fate of nations, a government that sets about this task calmly is clearly superior to one that insists on first going through a destructive and futile revolutionary attempt to avoid it.

THE APPLICABILITY OF LAROUI'S VISION

Important aspects of Laroui's theory appear to be validated by the research findings of other scholars as well as by events. Others have noted the leading role of the petite bourgeoisie in several revolutions. In her comparative study of the Iranian and Nicaraguan revolutions, Farideh Farhi noted that the "polar" classes (proletariat, peasantry, bourgeoisie) played a less important role than the "intermediate" classes (educated but impecunious professionals as well as the "petty [sic] bourgeoisie" (1990, 16–17, 37–41). In both cases, she notes, there were multiclass alliances that supported revolution. Forrest Colburn cited Cape Verde as a typical example of a Third World country that underwent Marxist revolution; the peasantry was not particularly revolutionary while in the cities there was no real bourgeoisie or proletariat, but there was a large petite bourgeoisie that supplied the revolutionary leadership (1994, 43–4).

Nazih Ayubi similarly argued that the main support for Islamic revolution in the Middle East does not come either from workers or peasants, but from intermediate classes, including the petite bourgeoisie, the "'new' middle strata," and students (1991, 158–63). He noted in particular that the "'virtually proletarianized members of the state-employed petite bourgeoisie, the under-employed intelligentsia, and the larger student population' are the main sponsors of the most militant of the Islamic tendencies" (161).

And just as Laroui did with regard to Arab nationalist regimes, others have observed the process of embourgeoisement occurring in other types of revolutionary regimes. Jerry Hough has described how Leninism appealed to the "half-peasants, half-workers of Russia" frightened of "westernization and those promoting it" in 1917. Over time, however, "the Westernized elite of Peter the Great" was recreated, resulting in the formation of a "huge middle class" that had "very different values from the peasants and workers who were its fathers and grandfathers" (1990, 10). By the 1980s,

> The broad educated public—the bureaucrats and the professionals— were eager for a relaxation of the dictatorship and an opening to the West. They were able to say that the closed nature of Soviet society was a central cause of the country's backwardness and a major threat to long-term defense. They could convincingly urge that what they wanted for themselves personally was absolutely necessary for the achievement of the most basic national goals (Hough 1990, 12).

Although he does not use this term, Hough described a process of gradual embourgeoisement of young Soviets from the 1950s onward. Far from being the initiator of embourgeoisement, Gorbachev (one of the 1950s youths) represented the culmination of pent-up demand for it.

Ervand Abrahamian observed this process at work shortly after the success of the Iranian revolution. He noted that during the early years of the revolution, Ayatollah Khomeini's populist rhetoric aroused anger "against the propertied middle classes" (1993, 51). Later, though, Khomeini emphasized that the middle class was, in fact, the backbone of the regime. On one occasion, for example, he stated that while parliamentary deputies "should always help" the lower class, they "must come predominantly from" the middle class: "'The revolution will remain secure,' Khomeini concluded, 'so long as the Parliament and the government are manned by members of the middle class'" (1993, 53). Abrahamian concluded that, "Although Khomeini has often been hailed as the champion of the deprived masses, his own words show him to be much more the spokesman of the propertied middle class" (1993, 58). Since the death of Khomeini, Iran's embourgeoisement has only accelerated as a result of the Rafsanjani government's emphasis on private investment and the overwhelming voter preference for a perceived moderate and liberal, Khatami, over a hard-line revolutionary purist, Nateq-Noori, in the 1997 presidential elections ("Islam and the Ballot Box" 1997).

Indeed, the past decade in particular has witnessed the rapid embourgeoisement of a remarkable number of revolutionary regimes. Several countries in Eastern Europe that had previously been ruled by hard-line Marxist-Leninist regimes have firmly embraced both liberal democracy and a free-market economy: Poland, the Czech Republic, Hungary, Romania, Slovenia, the Baltic states, and most dramatically, former East Germany and its voluntary absorption into a united Germany dominated by the former West. Indeed, the embourgeoisement of these countries has been so all-pervasive that in some of them, former communists have been elected back into office who, far from seeking to reverse this process, have sought to enhance and even accelerate it (Gebicki and Gebicki 1995).

It is hardly surprising, of course, that the embourgeoisement of Eastern Europe would occur so rapidly. Except for Yugoslavia and Albania, these nations did not experience indigenous Marxist-Leninist revolutions, but had Marxist-Leninist regimes imposed upon them by the USSR. For East Europeans—even former communists—getting rid of Marxism-Leninism was part and parcel of getting rid of foreign domination. Yet embourgeoisement has also proceeded rapidly in the former USSR—particularly Russia—where the original Marxist-Leninist revolution took place.

Unlike most of Eastern Europe, some of the strongest Russian political parties—including the communist one—are openly hostile to democracy. Boris Yeltsin—widely touted as a democrat in the period just before and after the collapse of the USSR—has resorted to the use of force against his political opponents on more than one occasion. Nevertheless, contested elections and a free press have become an established feature of post-Soviet Russian politics (White *et al.,* 1997). And while the commitment of the former communists in the Yeltsin regime to democracy may be questionable, their commitment to capitalism is not. It is the former communist enterprise managers—not the dissidents—who have overseen the considerable (though far from complete) capitalist transformation in Russia. These managers have, of course, used their position to acquire for themselves much of the equity in these privatized state enterprises. Having done so, however, it is these embourgeoised former communists who now have the greatest stake in the development of a capitalist economy domestically as well as collaboration with Western multinational corporations ("In Search of Spring" 1997). However much or little democratization has occurred elsewhere in the former Soviet Union, the ex-communist rulers of most former Soviet republics have also embraced—and personally benefited from—embourgeoisement.[2]

Chinese society has experienced a rapidly expanding embourgeoisement ever since Mao's successor, Deng Xiaoping, initiated capitalist economic transformation in the late 1970s. The Marxist leadership has been unwilling to allow democratization, but, as in Russia, it has a large personal stake in the continuation and expansion of a capitalist economy and trade with the West (Overholt 1996; Chan and Senser 1997). A similar process has been launched by the Marxist rulers of Vietnam (Elliott 1995). Whether or not they have made any progress toward democratization, most other former Marxist states in the Third World have also embarked on the path of embourgeoisement (Colburn 1994, 89–96). Indeed, there are only a handful of Marxist regimes that have not.

As Laroui himself noted, embourgeoisement has occurred—at least at the elite level—in some Arab nationalist revolutionary regimes. Egypt has advanced the farthest along this route: while its process of privatization has been relatively slow, this has accelerated in recent years ("The Retreat of Egypt's Islamists" 1997). And no matter how anti-Western oil-rich Arab nationalist regimes have been, none of them has been unwilling to sell their oil to the West—though certain Western countries (most notably the United States) have been unwilling to buy it.

Another example of an embourgeoised revolutionary regime is Mexico. After decades of maintaining a policy of nationalization of major industries and economic isolation from the United States, a new leadership generation in Mexico's ruling party—educated largely in the United States—began in the 1980s to pursue a policy of privatization and economic integration with the United States, culminating with Mexico joining the United States and Canada in the North American Free Trade Agreement (NAFTA), and an increasing degree of democratization (Castaneda 1996; Dresser 1997).

The near universality of revolutionary regimes embracing embourgeoisement in recent years suggests that this process is part of their normal evolution and not something exceptional. Indeed, the fact that there are only a handful of revolutionary regimes that have failed to undergo embourgeoisement indicates that these are somehow abnormal cases. These include, to a greater or lesser extent, Cuba, North Korea, Cambodia, Iraq, Libya, Sudan, Afghanistan, Tajikistan, and Belarus.

How have these states managed to avoid embourgeoisement, at least so far? Some have been unable to pursue it due to chronic civil war severely limiting private investment and consuming most government resources in military expenditures, such as in Cambodia, Sudan, Afghanistan, and Tajikistan. It is not clear, however, that all revolutionary regimes experiencing civil war at present would pursue embourgeoisement even if they succeeded in defeating their domestic opponents. And some not experiencing civil war have basically refused to permit embourgeoisement (Cuba, North Korea, Iraq, Libya, and Belarus). In most of these cases, a very strong leader—often the initiator of the revolution—has remained faithful to what Laroui would call his original petit bourgeois revolutionary vision, and strong enough to enforce it. Such has been the case with Fidel Castro in Cuba, Kim Il Sung (before his death) in North Korea, Saddam Hussein in Iraq, Mu'ammar al-Qadhafi in Libya, and Hasan Turabi in Sudan. This is significant, because in virtually all cases where revolutionary regimes have embraced embourgeoisement, this has not been done by the initial revolutionary leadership, but by its successors. Whether or not the successors to Castro, Hussein, al-Qadhafi, or Turabi pursue embourgeoisement—assuming that their regimes survive to be passed on to successors—remains to be seen.

Two cases appear somewhat anomalous. Although a successor leader, North Korea's Kim Jong Il has not retreated from his father's revolutionary fervor or permitted embourgeoisement. This may be because he is fearful that any change along these lines might unleash political forces he cannot control (Noland 1997).

Belarus's Alexander Lukashenka is hardly the originator of a revolution, or a figure with any sort of charisma. Unlike virtually all other post-Soviet leaders, however, he has been adamantly unwilling to allow embourgeoisement to proceed in his society. His goal appears to be to keep himself as well as Belarus's uncompetitive Soviet-era economic managers in power through convincing Russia to underwrite them financially. But as the Russian government has demonstrated its unwillingness to do this, and as Belarus becomes increasingly impoverished while its neighbors prosper (Markus 1996), it appears that Lukashenka—or more probably, a successor to him—will have to change course.

Revolutionary regimes that have not experienced embourgeoisement, then, seem to be special cases. There appears to be no permanent obstacle to their eventually embarking along this route once their civil wars come to an end, successor leaderships come to power, or a sufficient amount of time passes necessary for disillusionment with the original revolutionary vision to develop.

IMPLICATIONS OF LAROUI'S THEORY

Laroui's theory indicates that "petit bourgeois" revolutionary regimes eventually embrace embourgeoisement in the sense that they come to see privatization of their economies and cooperation with the West as being in their interest. Although embourgeoisement does not necessarily imply democratization, the former can precede or even be accompanied by the latter. The fact that most revolutionary regimes that were once hostile to the West and to market economics are now, irrespective of the extent to which they have democratized, pursuing cooperation with the West and marketization suggests that Laroui's theory is a powerful explanation of the evolution of revolutionary regimes.

What Laroui's theory implies is that, just as previous revolutionary regimes have done, revolutionary regimes that are now extremely hostile to the West will eventually embrace embourgeoisement and cooperation with the West. This would suggest, then, that we may look forward to the day when the Islamic Republic of Iran will drop its anti-American stance and seek cooperation with the United States instead. Indeed, Iran can already be said to be in the process of embourgeoisement, since the private sector plays an important role in the Iranian economy, Tehran cooperates with virtually all Western states except the United States, and competitive (if not completely free) elections play an increasingly important role in Iranian politics.

Further, Laroui's theory implies that anti-Western "petit bourgeois" revolutions occurring in the future will also experience embourgeoisement eventually. The one country in which Western governments as a group fear the consequences of revolution the most is Saudi Arabia. An anti-Western revolutionary regime here could limit Western access to Saudi petroleum, thus dramatically driving up the price of oil and seriously damaging Western economies. Laroui's theory, however, would indicate that no matter how anti-Western a revolutionary regime overthrowing the Saudis might be at first, it will eventually see cooperation with the West as being in its interests. Indeed, the fact that such vehemently anti-Western revolutionary leaders as Mu'ammar al-Qadhafi, Saddam

Hussein, and the Ayatollah Khomeini were always willing to sell oil to the West suggests that a revolutionary regime in Saudi Arabia would too; it would, after all, need the money.

Laroui's theory further implies that permanent hostility on the part of Western states toward revolutionary regimes—such as the United States has shown to Iran—may actually be counterproductive. While revolutionary regimes are likely to be highly anti-Western in their early, petit bourgeois phase, Western governments need to be aware that the embourgeoisement of such regimes is part of their natural evolution. Implacable Western hostility to such regimes may unnecessarily delay or prolong this process. This is the gist of the argument currently being made by some former American foreign-policymakers criticizing the U.S. government's continuing hostility toward Iran despite numerous signs of that country's retreat from revolutionary fervor (Brzezinski et al. 1997; Murphy 1997).

Nevertheless, Laroui's theory does not imply that the West should be complacent about anti-Western petit bourgeois revolutions, since they are destined to evolve into embourgeoised pro-Western regimes in the long run. There are two problems with Laroui's theory that unsettle this optimistic conclusion. First, Laroui does not indicate whether there is any particular time frame in which the embourgeoisement of revolutionary regimes can be expected to occur. And as the actual experience of such regimes shows, this process can take a very long time indeed—seven decades in the case of the Soviet Union. The status quo Western powers can hardly be expected to forego trying to stop a revolutionary regime from attempting to export anti-Western revolution (if that is what it is trying to do) due to the conviction that it will eventually abandon such efforts as it undergoes embourgeoisement. Indeed, Western efforts to frustrate the attempt to export revolution may play an important role in convincing revolutionary regimes to abandon this and other revolutionary goals as well as embark upon embourgeoisement.

The fact that the embourgeoisement of a revolutionary regime may not begin, much less be completed, for a relatively long period of time poses a problem for Western foreign-policymakers. They will oppose revolutionary regimes that, in their petit bourgeois phase, seek to export revolution. On the other hand, they should be prepared to collaborate with revolutionary regimes embarking upon embourgeoisement. These phases, however, may overlap, such as when a "moderate" faction in a revolutionary regime embarks on embourgeoisement domestically while an "extremist" faction continues the policy of attempting to export revolution—as appears to be occurring in Iran. Such a situation calls for a nuanced policy on the part of the West that demonstrates its determination to thwart the export of revolution but also encourages embourgeoisement so that the "moderates" within the revolutionary regime can credibly argue that the West is not implacably hostile and that cooperation with it is possible. Such a policy, of course, is extremely difficult to devise and sustain, especially when there are strong domestic political pressures favoring one policy extreme. While American foreign-policymakers and businessmen may increasingly favor a friendlier U.S. policy toward Iran, the Republican-controlled Congress and American public opinion in general is unprepared to pursue anything except a hard-line policy toward that country at present (Morgan and Ottaway 1997).

The second problem with Laroui's theory is a more important one. Laroui appears to suggest that once a revolutionary regime embraces embourgeoisement, then embourgeoisement will occur. But while this might be a necessary condition for embourgeoisement to take place, it is not a sufficient one. In order for this project to succeed, society in a revolutionary regime must be willing to embrace embourgeoisement despite the economic hardships it inevitably gives rise to. And experience has shown that not all societies are as willing to do this as others.

The societies that have most enthusiastically embraced embourgeoisement are those in most of the Eastern European nations as well as China. And in these countries, embourgeoisement appears to be secure; it seems highly unlikely that forces seeking to destroy free-market economies will rise up in these nations, despite the significant economic dislocations they have experienced.

Mexican society has exhibited a somewhat lesser degree of enthusiasm for the rigors of the free market. One of the political parties that did especially well in the 1997 parliamentary and Mexico City mayoralty elections was the leftist Party of the Democratic Revolution. Its egalitarian and nationalistic economic policies appeal to many of those who have been hurt by Mexico opening itself to economic competition from the United States and Canada through NAFTA. Should this party's candidate win the presidential elections, it is not clear that Mexico would remain as committed to NAFTA as the recent reformist Institutional Revolutionary Party (PRI) governments have been. On the other hand, Mexico's other leading opposition party, the National Action Party, appears to be at least as committed as the PRI to open markets and free trade with the United States ("Mexico Enters the Era of Politics" 1997).

A country in which a wide gap has developed between the government's and a significant segment of society's degree of commitment to embourgeoisement is Russia. There are powerful communist and nationalist parties that have vociferously denounced the extent to which the Yeltsin government has pursued economic privatization and cooperation with the West. If either of these parties captured the Russian presidency, they may well attempt not just to halt but to reverse what progress has been made toward embourgeoisement. Survey research, however, shows that attitudes toward the free market and cooperation with the West tend to divide along generational lines in Russia. It is primarily the older generation that opposes and the younger generation that supports embourgeoisement (Dobson 1996, 10). Assuming that the younger people in Russia now embracing embourgeoisement do not renounce it as they grow older, the passage of time should lead to steadily decreasing support for political parties opposed to it.

The countries where there appears to be an especially wide gap between the government's and society's commitment to embourgeoisement are the postrevolutionary Arab nationalist states—especially Egypt. This is ironic, because it was Egypt in particular where Laroui expected embourgeoisement to proceed as the government became increasingly committed to it. But in Egypt and most other postrevolutionary Arab nationalist regimes, there have arisen powerful Islamic fundamentalist groups generally opposed to embourgeoisement. As noted earlier, several observers have described the main supporters of these movements as hailing from the petite bourgeoisie—the group that supported Arab nationalist revolution to begin with. And unlike in Russia, the younger generation is the basis of support and leadership for these opposition movements in the Arab world (Roy 1994, 49–55).

There are several possible explanations as to why some societies are extremely willing to embrace embourgeoisement while others are resistant to it. Some might cite complex cultural and historical factors. Others might see a society's level of education as having a strong impact on both its willingness and its ability to embrace embourgeoisement. Others still might see the manner in which the government pursues embourgeoisement as being the primary determinant of society's reaction to it: if embourgeoisement is carried out inefficiently and appears to benefit only certain privileged groups, it should hardly be surprising if society as a whole does not support it. Jack Goldstone has suggested that population pressures may impede even good-faith efforts by developing countries to promote prosperity, thus leading to the revolutionary situations they seek to avoid (Goldstone 1997).

Discovering precisely why some societies are not amenable to embourgeoisement at present, though, is less important for purposes of this study than the observation that their being so—for whatever reason—can have consequences that Laroui did not anticipate. In Laroui's terms, a petit bourgeois revolutionary regime that itself becomes embourgeoised but that fails to embourgeoise the petit bourgeois society it rules over may find itself the target of revolutionary forces arising from that society. Instead of merely postponing embourgeoisement, the original petit bourgeois revolution may eventually lead to yet another petit bourgeois revolution—which in turn must go through the time-consuming process of becoming embourgeoised itself before it too can try (and possibly fail) to embourgeoise society.

Thus, in Egypt and Algeria, embourgeoised Arab nationalist regimes that have failed to embourgeoise society are being challenged by "petit bourgeois" Islamic fundamentalist revolutionaries. If these groups come to power and also fail to embourgeoise society, they too may eventually discredit themselves and be opposed and even overthrown by another generation of revolutionaries. It is also possible that Islamic fundamentalist regimes may prove more successful at embourgeoising countries than the Arab nationalist regimes they might overthrow. And it is even possible that the present Arab nationalist regimes that have so far failed to embourgeoise their societies may somehow succeed in doing this—though as Islamic fundamentalist opposition to them mounts, this appears to be increasingly unlikely.

Laroui's theory of revolution does not foretell which—if any— of these alternatives will occur in postrevolutionary states. His theory, though, is useful for understanding how the decision by revolutionary regimes to embark on embourgeoisement is a normal part of their postrevolutionary evolution. The problems with his theory examined here, however, illustrate how the decision by a revolutionary regime to pursue embourgeoisement may not necessarily be successfully implemented.

Part II

NATIONALISM AND REVOLUTION

CHAPTER 3

RESSENTIMENT AND REVOLUTION
Reflections on Liah Greenfeld

IN HER BOOK *NATIONALISM: Five Roads to Modernity* (1992), Liah Greenfeld discussed the central role played by *ressentiment* (resentment) in fostering nationalism. She described how ressentiment can arise from the growing perception in one nation that it was "falling behind" others. This chapter will explore how the concept of ressentiment can be applied to the study of revolution. In doing so, however, it will show how the study of revolution necessitates certain modifications in the concept of ressentiment as expounded by Greenfeld. In short, this chapter will examine what ressentiment tells us about revolution, and what revolution tells us about ressentiment.

GREENFELD'S CONCEPT OF RESSENTIMENT

Greenfeld's book described the development of nationalism in five countries: England, France, Russia, Germany, and the United States. For Greenfeld, there are basically two types of nationalism: civic and ethnic. Civic nationalism is inclusive: it is open to different ethnic groups residing in the territory of the state, and even to immigrants in its most liberal variation. Ethnic nationalism, by contrast, is exclusive: it is closed to everyone except members of a specific ethnic group. Others residing in the territory of the state are excluded, as are immigrants (unless, of course, they also belong to the favored ethnic group). Greenfeld saw England and the United States as examples of the development of civic nationalism while Russia and Germany were examples of the development of ethnic nationalism. She described France as a mixed case, but with features making its nationalism more akin to the ethnic nationalist variety.

Greenfeld described ressentiment as being an essential feature in the development of nationalism:

> Every society importing the foreign idea of the nation inevitably focused on the source of importation—an object of imitation by definition—and reacted to it. Because the model was superior to the imitator in the latter's own perception (its being a model implied that), and the contact itself more often than not served to emphasize the latter's inferiority, the reaction commonly assumed the form of *ressentiment*. . . . *[R]essentiment* refers to a psychological state resulting from suppressed feelings of envy and hatred (existential envy) and the impossibility of satisfying these feelings. The sociological basis for *ressentiment*—or the structural conditions that are necessary for the development of this psychological state—is twofold. The first condition . . . is the fundamental comparability between the subject and the object of envy, or rather the belief on the part of the subject in the fundamental equality between them, which makes them in principle interchangeable. The second condition is the actual inequality (perceived as not fundamental) of such dimensions that it rules out practical achievement of the theoretically existing equality. The presence of these conditions renders a situation *ressentiment*-prone. . . . (1992, 15–16)

According to Greenfeld, ressentiment directed toward other states is an especially important feature in the development of ethnic nationalism. She then went on to argue that French nationalist ressentiment was directed toward England, which had displaced France as the most powerful European nation over the course of the eighteenth century (177–84); Russian nationalist ressentiment was directed at the West as a whole for being "ahead" of Russia (222–35); and German nationalist ressentiment was directed first against France, then Britain, and then the United States when each of these was in turn the leading power (371–86).

Further, Greenfeld saw the ressentiment of states possessing ethnic nationalism as being highly resistant to change. Writing in the wake of the downfall of communism, she warned that the adoption of capitalism would not necessarily lead to the adoption of democracy, since capitalism "can very well coexist with societies which are anything but democratic" (489). She further warned that, "So long as the national identity remains unchanged, the fundamental structure of motivations and, consequently, the fundamental nature of the national society remain unchanged, and patterns of behavior characteristic of it in the past should be expected" (490). This implies that even democratization cannot be depended upon to alter the ressentiment that states imbued with ethnic nationalism harbor toward other states. If ethnic nationalist states are not pursuing ressentiment-inspired objectives, this is not necessarily due to lack of motive, but merely to the absence of "propitious conditions." If conditions change but motivations do not, "the potential for their realization exists" (490).

By contrast, Greenfeld did not see ressentiment directed toward other states as an important element in England or the United States, the two cases of civic nationalism that she examined. This was true in England due to its being, in her view, the first country to develop modern nationalism. There being no foreign model of nationalism to imitate, ressentiment in seventeenth-century England was not directed at other countries, but exclusively against the internal "society of orders." Nevertheless, she saw civic nationalism in general as not being prone to ressentiment toward other countries. With regard to the United States—the nation that she considered to be the purest embodiment of civic nationalism—she wrote, "American national identity was not sustained by the hatred of the other; it knew no *ressentiment*" (422).

THE PRESENCE OF
RESSENTIMENT IN REVOLUTION

Although Greenfeld did not write about revolution specifically, it would appear that her concept of ressentiment could be utilized to elucidate our understanding of this phenomenon, since revolution is often the culmination of intense feelings of nationalism. Indeed, revolution occurred in all five countries whose nationalism she examined. As she herself argued, ressentiment against foreign states played an important role in the French, Russian, and German cases.

Anticolonial revolution, by definition, arises from ressentiment against foreign rule. Despite Greenfeld's general statement about the absence of ressentiment in American nationalism, her own description of the American Revolution indicates that there was a significant element of ressentiment directed at Britain by the time it began (416–21).

But even revolution in independent countries often possesses a strong element of ressentiment directed against foreign powers. During the Cold War, for example, revolutionaries fighting against right-wing dictatorships in the Third World usually felt intense ressentiment toward the United States for supporting these regimes. Indeed, American support to them may have contributed to the decision by their domestic opponents to become Marxist, thereby positioning themselves (they hoped) to receive support from the USSR—America's most powerful challenger during this period (MacFarlane 1985, 202–3).

Arab nationalist revolutionaries in the 1950s and 1960s felt intense ressentiment toward Britain and France for having divided the Arab world into separate states and for installing pro-Western regimes in these artificially created entities when they ended their colonial rule, and toward the United States for its support to Israel and conservative Arab regimes (Dawisha 1986, 16–26).

The Islamic fundamentalist revolutionaries who came to power in Iran in 1979 were also motivated by intense ressentiment toward the United States for having supported the autocratic rule of the Shah (Bakhash 1990, 70, 237). Islamic fundamentalist revolutionaries now operating in several Arab states are similarly motivated by ressentiment toward the United States for its support both to the dictatorial regimes they are trying to oust and to Israel (Karabell 1996–97).

America and the West, however, have not been the only targets of Muslim ressentiment: the *mujahadin*—the Islamic holy warriors— who fought against the Marxist regime in Afghanistan during the 1980s felt intense ressentiment toward the USSR for militarily intervening to protect it (Roy 1994, 157). Similarly, the East European democratic revolutionaries of 1989 were motivated by ressentiment toward the USSR—the power that imposed Marxist-Leninist regimes on them at the end of World War II (Brzezinski 1989, 106).

Ressentiment directed at powerful foreign states, then, has been a common feature of modern revolution. Indeed, it is difficult to think of any cases in the twentieth century (and most of those before it) where this feature has not been present.

There is one important difference, though, in the ressentiment Greenfeld attributed to nationalists and that actually experienced by revolutionaries. Greenfeld wrote that a source of frustration for nationalists is their inability to achieve the equality they believe is "theoretically existing" between their nation and the object of their ressentiment. Actual revolutionaries, by contrast, believe that it is possible to rectify this imbalance beginning (though not always ending) with a successful revolution.

WHAT RESSENTIMENT TELLS
US ABOUT REVOLUTION

Those who make revolution do not just have domestic ambitions, but international ones as well. In addition to overthrowing the existing regime and replacing it with another, revolutionaries have sought to enhance the international status of their country. The minimum international goal of anticolonial "nationalist" revolutionaries has been to expel foreign rule from their country and establish independent statehood. The maximum goal of revolutionaries has been to establish their nation as a great power. Whether they are minimal or maximal, however, these international goals of revolutionaries can, as indicated earlier, be seen as having been inspired by ressentiment.

How successful have revolutionaries been at achieving their international goals? And what happens to a nation's sense of ressentiment over time? These questions will first be looked at with regard to the minimum international goal—independence—and then with regard to more ambitious international goals.

Ressentiment and "Minimum Goal" Revolutions

Not all revolutionaries who have fought for independence have achieved it. But since the eighteenth century, almost all nations that have achieved independence through revolution have kept it. Of course, there have been many nations that have achieved independence peacefully, without revolution, and that have remained independent. The latter may have been assisted in achieving independence peacefully through the actions of those who achieved it via revolution, helping to convince West European publics and governments that the costs of continued rule over colonies desiring independence were prohibitively high.

Perhaps ressentiment against foreign rule can be said to have been stronger among those nations that fought for their independence than those that didn't but achieved it anyway. It seems reasonable to assume, however, that ressentiment against foreign rule is sufficiently strong in virtually all independent states—no matter how independence was achieved—that they would resist the forcible reimposition of foreign rule. Indeed, ressentiment against foreign rule is so great that, with one exception—Newfoundland (Salloum 1995)—no state that has achieved independence has voluntarily surrendered it in the twentieth century. Nor do many more appear likely to.[1] Nations seeking the minimum goal of independence, at least from West European rule, have been highly successful both in achieving their goal and in maintaining it afterward.

But if establishing or affirming independence is the only international goal of revolutionaries, ressentiment toward foreign powers— even the former colonial power—does not usually persist. In the case of former colonies that achieved it relatively peacefully, ressentiment usually does not persist to any meaningful extent after the achievement of independence. Indeed, considering the hatred for colonialism among nations while they were experiencing it, after their independence there has been a surprising degree of cooperation (alongside a certain degree of contention) between Britain and those of its former colonies that joined the Commonwealth (the majority), and an extraordinary degree of cooperation between France and its former colonies in sub-Saharan Africa (Low 1991, 331–8).

The experience of mutual antagonism during an anticolonial revolution has often served to fuel the continuation of ressentiment toward the ex-colonial power for many years after a country's independence. Nevertheless, this ressentiment has often receded and even given way to close cooperation between former antagonists. Despite the American Revolution and the War of 1812, British-American relations became reasonably cooperative throughout the rest of the nineteenth century, and extremely close during the twentieth (Greenfeld 1992, 421; Howard 1995).

The case of Ireland is even more dramatic. Despite centuries of Irish nationalist ressentiment toward harsh British rule, the government that emerged in Dublin following the Irish Revolution has had remarkably pacific and even (since Ireland's 1973 accession to the European Community) cooperative relations with London, despite continued British rule in Ulster (Keatinge 1983; Arthur 1996).

Despite the fierce wars waged by Portugal against the revolutionaries seeking independence for them, relations between Lisbon and all of its ex-colonies in Africa are now very friendly (Cardoso 1994).

Although Algerian nationalist ressentiment toward France was very strong both during and for some time after the Algerian Revolution, France has become the closest ally of the military regime that inherited power from the nationalists in its ongoing struggle against Islamic fundamentalist revolutionaries (Serfaty 1996–97).

Revolutionaries fighting for independence, then, feel intense ressentiment toward the colonial power they are fighting against before achieving independence, and sometimes even afterward. Sooner or later (more often sooner in the cases cited here), however, this ressentiment toward the former colonial power diminishes to the point where close cooperation with it becomes possible. For revolutions that just seek the minimum international goal of establishing a country's independence, ressentiment toward the former colonial power tends to diminish once this goal has been achieved.

Ressentiment and "Maximum Goal" Revolutions

Independence, of course, has not been the only international goal of revolutionaries. Whether or not a nation was already independent, some revolutionaries have sought to establish—or more often, reestablish—the great power status of their nation. It is remarkable that a number of revolutions with the most ambitious international goals have taken place in countries that had once been great powers but that subsequently experienced significant decline.

In such cases, ressentiment over the loss of a nation's great power status is directed not only toward other nations that have become more powerful, but toward the ancien régime for having "allowed" this to happen—thus providing additional justification for the necessity of its overthrow. This was true in France, Russia, and Germany—the three cases of nationalism where Greenfeld saw ressentiment directed toward other states. France's decline in power vis-à-vis England over the course of the eighteenth century contributed to the delegitimization of the French monarchy (Stone 1994). Similarly, Russia's humiliating defeat by Japan in 1905 and extremely poor showing against Germany in World War I served to undermine tsarist rule (Treadgold 1990, 54, 98–102). In Germany, ressentiment over the terms of the 1919 Versailles Treaty, including the loss of a significant amount of German territory to other states, served to undermine the Weimar Republic and fuel the Nazi cause (Carsten 1971, 90, 134).

Ressentiment over the loss of great power status was also present in several other revolutions. Despite being on the winning side in World War I, the Italian constitutional monarchy's inability to be awarded more than relatively modest territorial gains by its more powerful allies contributed to its delegitimization and to the growth of Mussolini's fascist movement (Carsten 1971, 48–9). In China, the failure of the imperial government to halt the encroachments of foreign powers contributed to its delegitimization and the rise to power of the Kuomintang (Hsu 1970, 430–2, 527–37). But then, the

Kuomintang's ineffectiveness against invasion by Japan contributed in turn to its delegitimization and the rise to power of the Chinese Communist Party (Johnson 1962, 31–70). The subservience of the Egyptian and Iraqi monarchies to Britain contributed to their delegitimization and overthrow by Arab nationalist revolutionaries (Kerr 1971, 1–5). Similarly, the subservience of the Shah's government to the United States contributed to its delegitimization and overthrow by Islamic fundamentalist revolutionaries (Munson 1988, 122–3).

Like revolutionaries seeking the minimum goal of independence, those pursuing the maximum international goal of restoring their nation's great power status are optimistic that they can accomplish this task. But there is an important difference between them. For those pursuing independence alone, its achievement marks the end of the revolution and the point at which ressentiment directed at the former colonial power begins to diminish. But for those pursuing the restoration of a nation's great power status, the coming to power of a new regime alone does not achieve this maximum goal. To do this, the new regime must undertake a series of actions designed to strengthen itself and weaken the states toward which it feels ressentiment. And, as numerous historians and international relations theorists have pointed out, the more aggressively a state pursues great power ambitions, the more likely it is to meet with resistance from other states (Morgenthau 1973, 167–77; Kennedy 1987). Unlike those revolutionaries who just seek independence, the ressentiment of those who pursue the restoration of their country's great power status does not necessarily diminish after they come to power. As they experience frustration in achieving their great power ambitions, their ressentiment can increase. Or more dramatically, the initial success of revolutionary regimes in achieving more modest great power goals can lead to contempt for their enemies (or revolutionary hubris), which in turn leads to the pursuit of far more ambitious objectives. A heightened degree of ressentiment develops when the pursuit of such ambitions brings about the inevitable alliance of other states determined to prevent their achievement, as occurred when the French and German revolutions gave rise to Napoleon's and Hitler's efforts to conquer Europe; the Bolshevik revolution led to Stalin's forceful imposition of Marxist rule in Eastern Europe and later Khrushchev's and Brezhnev's support for revolution in the Third World; 'Abd al-Nasir's "victory" over the British, French, and Israelis in 1956 led to his attempt to unite the entire Arab world into one United Arab Republic; and, after successfully repulsing the Iraqi invasion of Iran, Ayatollah Khomeini attempted to overthrow the regime of Saddam Hussein and establish an Islamic Republic of Iraq under Iranian auspices.

But while ressentiment toward other states may burn more intensely within revolutionary regimes that pursue maximum international goals after they come to power than in those that pursue minimum ones, it can also abruptly diminish in the former—especially as a result of military defeat.

Perhaps the most dramatic examples of this were post–World War II West Germany, Italy, and Japan, where not just the governments renounced ressentiment-based great power ambitions, but the general publics in these countries did so as well. In both West Germany and Japan, a strong sense of pacifism developed after World War II and has remained strong ever since (Ruehl 1992, 105–7; Sasae 1994, 14–18). Ultra-nationalist groups are present to a greater or lesser extent in these countries, but are only a minority phenomena in them. At present, it appears absolutely unthinkable that ressentiment-inspired revolutionaries could ever organize a successful revolutionary movement in any of these three countries and embark on a militaristic effort to reassert their countries' lost great power status. The knowledge that the pursuit of these maximum goals brought disaster and defeat to their countries serves as a powerful disincentive to any further effort to achieve them.

By contrast, ressentiment toward other countries did persist in France after its final defeat in the Napoleonic wars. But French ressentiment was not so much aimed at reviving France as *the* great power but as *a* great power in order to protect itself from Germany. Even then, it was not able to prevent itself from being defeated in the Franco-Prussian War, having much of its territory devastated in World War I, and being defeated as well as occupied in World War II—all at the hands of Germany. Following World War II, France's failed military efforts first to restore its colonial empire in Indochina and then retain it in Algeria were motivated to a significant degree by the desire to revive France's great power status. French withdrawal from NATO in the mid-1960s can also be seen as an expression of ressentiment directed at the United States. Paris's post–Cold War rapprochement with NATO, however, indicates that French ressentiment has diminished substantially since then (Grant 1996).

Egypt also abandoned its ressentiment-inspired great power ambitions after being defeated by Israel in the June 1967 War. After 'Abd al-Nasir's humiliating loss, he quickly ended his quarrel with the conservative Arab states. His successor, Anwar Sadat, gave up great power ambitions even further by establishing close relations with the United States and even making peace with Israel—policies his successor, Hosni Mubarak, has continued (Kerr 1971, 130; Dawisha 1986, 25). Nor does this seem likely to change as long as the present regime remains in power.

Similarly, though perhaps not as widely recognized, the Iranian failure to demolish the regime of Saddam Hussein in the long-drawn-out Iran-Iraq War appears to have contributed to a decline in Iranian ressentiment. Although still highly resentful of the United States, Khomeini's successors have sought cooperation with other Western states and have displayed a considerable degree of ambivalence toward Islamic fundamentalist revolutionaries in some countries such as Afghanistan and Tajikistan (Katz 1997, 75–81). The election of a "moderate" over a "hard-liner" as president in 1997 indicates that the Iranian public no longer values revolutionary purity or is as animated by ressentiment as it was during the late 1970s.

The collapse of communism and the breakup of the Soviet Union was an unusual case of how the pursuit of highly ambitious ressentiment-inspired goals was abruptly abandoned, as this did not occur as a direct result of military defeat. Although the Soviet stalemate in Afghanistan played a role in it, the collapse of communism appears to have occurred more as the unintended result of Mikhail Gorbachev's attempt to reform communism, and his unwillingness to use force to preserve the status quo after the consequences of his policies became increasingly clear (Rodman 1994, 289–323). What apparently underlay Gorbachev's actions was the conviction that, unlike his predecessors, he personally did not feel ressentiment toward the West or view it as posing a threat.

Since the breakup of the USSR, though, ressentiment toward other states appears to have been resurrected in Russia by the electorally powerful communist and nationalist parties as well as by the Yeltsin administration at times. For the most part, however, this ressentiment is not aimed at restoring the global superpower status of the former Soviet Union, but at the lesser goal of asserting Russia's role as the predominant power within the space of the former USSR and as a (and not *the*) great power in Eurasia generally (Pipes 1997). But Russia's humiliating defeat at the hands of the Chechens inside the boundaries of the Russian Federation itself has cast serious doubt on Russia's ability and willingness to pursue even modest ressentiment-inspired objectives outside those boundaries. Although some Western analysts see post-Soviet Russian nationalism as a precursor of renewed expansionism, Russian ressentiment may instead be experiencing a slow decline similar to French ressentiment after World War II in focusing on relatively modest goals but later abandoning even some of these.

But whether it occurs abruptly or slowly, the scaling back or abandonment of pretensions to being a great power is the signal that the ressentiment of a revolutionary regime pursuing maximum goals has either come to an end or been reduced to the point of meaninglessness. This process appears to be directly associated with military defeat in all but the Soviet/Russian case, though this factor was present in it as well.

Ressentiment and "Intermediate Goal" Revolutions

There has also been a curious group of revolutions whose international goals have fallen between the extremes of minimum and maximum discussed here. These are revolutionary regimes that have attempted to don the mantle of a great power in their region or even beyond, but have not attempted to do this independently (as would a revolutionary regime pursuing maximum international goals). They have instead attempted to play this role with the support, and as the junior partner, of a more powerful revolutionary regime pursuing maximum international goals.

This category includes several (though by no means all) Marxist-Leninist regimes in the Third World during the Cold War: North Korea, North Vietnam/Vietnam, and most of all, Cuba. Fascist Italy should also be included in this category, at least from the onset of World War II in 1939 to the downfall of Mussolini in 1943.

As the case of Mussolini shows, military defeat can bring an abrupt end to the ressentiment-inspired pursuit of intermediate international goals by a revolutionary regime. On the other hand, the Marxist Third World cases show that revolutionary "junior partners" can be shielded from the effects of military defeat or stalemate, allowing them to continue pursuing their intermediate international goals.

Despite the expulsion of its forces from South Korea and the fact that virtually all its territory was overrun by U.S./UN forces, military assistance from the USSR and China allowed North Korea not only to survive this defeat, but also to both retain its original ressentiment-inspired goal of reuniting the Korean Peninsula by force, as well as maintaining (again, with Soviet and Chinese assistance) a large enough military force to credibly threaten, if not actually launch such an attempt, for over four decades after the end of the Korean War (Robinson 1989, 187–93).

Primarily Soviet and secondarily Chinese military assistance to North Vietnam allowed Hanoi to, despite the enormous casualties it suffered, prevent the United States from defeating its forces and those of its allies elsewhere in Indochina until American forces were withdrawn as a result of the domestic political and economic turmoil in the United States that the war was causing. Later, Soviet military assistance allowed Vietnam to invade Cambodia, set up a regime allied to it there, and prosecute a counterinsurgency campaign against the Khmer Rouge (which its invasion had ousted) for over a decade despite its inability to defeat them (Pike 1987).

Soviet military assistance to Cuba allowed Castro to, among other feats, help the Popular Movement for the Liberation of Angola (MPLA) fend off attacks from U.S.- and white South African-backed rivals in Angola in 1975–76, check and roll back the Somali invasion of Ethiopia in 1977–78, militarily assist the Sandinistas in their overthrow of the Somoza regime in Nicaragua in 1979, and prosecute a counterinsurgency campaign against the MPLA's enemies in Angola despite its inability to defeat them (Katz 1997, 34–5, 71). Far more than North Korea and North Vietnam/Vietnam with their ambitions vis-à-vis neighboring states, Soviet assistance allowed Cuba to play the role of great power on two continents.

But if support from a larger revolutionary state allowed North Korea, North Vietnam/Vietnam, and Cuba to pursue their intermediate international goals despite military defeat or stalemate, the withdrawal of that support greatly altered their ability to do so despite the fact that the revolutionary regimes have survived (so far) the collapse of communism in all three countries. Without Soviet support, Vietnam withdrew its troops from Cambodia in 1989 and has essentially given up its ressentiment-inspired international goals in exchange for trade and investment from the West—including its once-hated enemy, the United States. Also without Soviet support, Cuba recalled its troops from abroad, and was unable to do anything to prevent the electoral defeat of the Sandinistas in Nicaragua, the military defeat of the Mengistu regime in Ethiopia, or the MPLA regime in Angola surviving in part through ingratiating itself with Castro's American enemies. The leaders of both North Korea and Cuba still appear to harbor ressentiment-inspired international goals; but without external support from more powerful revolutionary regimes, they are no longer in a position to pursue them. Their once mighty ressentiment has turned into impotent ressentiment (Katz 1997, 105–6).

WHAT REVOLUTION TELLS US ABOUT RESSENTIMENT

Contrary to Greenfeld's portrayal of it, studying revolutions and the evolution of revolutionary regimes afterward reveals that ressentiment is not static and unchanging once it develops. Ressentiment can rise up in a nation, but then it can—and usually does—decline in it as well. Further, ressentiment is not an undifferentiated feeling or force in those nations where it is present. In many countries, ressentiment has only sought the minimum goal of establishing a nation's independence and having it generally recognized. In others, however, the type of ressentiment that rises up demands the pursuit of more ambitious international goals. And the nature of a nation's ressentiment-inspired international goals has a strong impact on how, as well as how quickly, a nation's sense of ressentiment declines. As was shown here, the ressentiment of a nation pursuing only the minimum international goal of establishing its independence begins to recede once that goal has been achieved. But in countries where more ambitious international goals are pursued, ressentiment can increase even after a revolution (which is the culmination of the ressentiment-inspired domestic goal of ousting the ancien régime). Their ressentiment tends not to decline until it experiences some externally administered reversal such as military defeat or the withdrawal of great power support.

In addition, the study of how revolutionary regimes evolve casts doubt on Greenfeld's contention that ressentiment directed at other nations is solely the possession of states imbued with ethnic nationalism and not at all that of states with civic nationalism. Her own analysis of the French case indicates that there is not necessarily a sharp distinction between ethnic and civic nationalisms; elements of both can be present in one nation. And while there is some evidence to support her argument that her "purer" cases of civic nationalism (Britain and the United States) lack ressentiment toward other nations, there is simply not enough evidence to make this thesis truly convincing.

Obviously, these two states imbued with civic nationalism possess the minimum ressentiment necessary to assert independence (as the United States did in the American Revolution) or maintain it (as Britain did most notably during World War II). The real test of whether or not these states imbued with civic nationalism possess a lesser degree of ressentiment than states imbued with ethnic nationalism is whether there is a difference in how they respond to the loss of great power status.

Britain obviously possessed a sufficient degree of ressentiment to resist yielding its position as the predominant world power to

Napoleonic France, Imperial Germany, or Nazi Germany. Britain, however, did yield this position without contest to the United States after World War II. Nor has it attempted a ressentiment-inspired effort to regain its lost position (Howard 1995). At least with regard to other democracies, then, Greenfeld appears to be correct in portraying Britain as lacking ressentiment toward other states.

It is not yet known, however, whether or not the United States would exhibit ressentiment over the loss of great power status for the simple reason that this has not yet occurred. It does not seem likely that the American government and public would be indifferent to the loss of American preeminence. On the other hand, even in the wake of the successful American-led effort to expel Iraqi forces from Kuwait, survey data indicate that the American public supports the use of force only under limited circumstances and would probably not be willing to pay a very high price to pursue ambitious ressentiment-inspired goals (Jentleson 1992).

The British and the American cases alone do not provide a sufficient basis to confidently make statements about the relationship between civic nationalism and ressentiment. It should be noted, though, that just as the excesses of ethnic nationalism are not necessarily a permanent characteristic of a nation that once experienced them (as Germany shows), the virtues of civic nationalism do not always last either. The breakup of both the Soviet Union and Yugoslavia are evidence that the attempt by nondemocratic revolutionary regimes to create a civic nationalism unifying disparate ethnic groups can backfire and actually serve to intensify previously existing antagonisms, or even create them. Nor does the existence of even a relatively long-established democracy guarantee that the civic nationalism it attempts to foster does not succumb to the rise of ethnic nationalism, as the growth of Hindu fundamentalism in India and the persistence of Quebec separatism in Canada demonstrate.

CONCLUSION

The study of revolutions and the evolution of revolutionary regimes afterward indicates several ways in which Greenfeld's concept of ressentiment needs to be modified. With these modifications, though, the concept of ressentiment is an extremely useful one not only for explaining the international goals of revolutionaries and revolutionary regimes in the past and present, but also for assessing their potential in the future.

For example, while the age of West European colonialism is now largely over and the few remaining such colonies tend to be tiny territories with small populations that do not want independence, sensitivity to ressentiment would suggest that there is still an enormous potential for revolution seeking the minimum ressentiment-inspired goal of independence. This phenomenon, often called "separatism" by outsiders but seen as nationalist revolution by those seeking it, is currently evident in Chechnya, Tibet, Xinjiang, Kashmir, the Tamil regions of Sri Lanka, Kurdistan, southern Sudan (Equatoria), several parts of Ethiopia, Mindinao, and elsewhere. It is not clear whether the revolutionaries fighting for independence will ever achieve it for these regions. But so far, many governments have been unable to suppress them even after trying to do so for years or even decades. Further, the breakup of the USSR, Yugoslavia, Czechoslovakia, and Ethiopia at the end of the Cold War has only served to encourage such movements elsewhere by providing successful role models. For if small nations could secede from all these countries—especially one as powerful as the former Soviet Union—why can't secession occur elsewhere? Whether they succeed or not, there is no reason to think that the ressentiment of revolutionaries fighting against overland colonialism will be any less intense than that of previous revolts against overseas colonialism.

In addition, there is one extant case of a revolutionary regime pursuing great power ambitions in a country imbued with ethnic nationalism that has not yet experienced a diminution in its ressentiment against other states: China. Ressentiment directed against the United States in particular was a significant component of the ideology espoused by Mao Zedong during the years he was in power (Van Ness 1970, 24–35). While the tenets of Maoist ideology have either been abandoned or rendered meaningless through the steady construction of a capitalist economy under the leadership of Deng Xiaoping and his successors, the one aspect of

Maoism that has remained salient in China, both inside the regime and among the general populace, is ressentiment toward the West in general and America in particular (Shambaugh 1994, 49–51; Bernstein and Munro 1997). The experience of other ethnic nationalist states that pursue ressentiment-inspired great power ambitions ominously suggests that, unless China undergoes an internal political transformation similar to that which occurred under Gorbachev in the USSR, China's ressentiment is not likely to diminish until it suffers a humiliating military defeat.

Finally, it appears that ressentiment directed toward other states is just as likely to animate revolutionaries and revolutionary regimes in the future as it has done in the past. Those seeking to understand the complex, multifaceted phenomenon of revolution will need to understand the role that ressentiment plays in it.

CHAPTER 4

RELATIVE DEPRIVATION IN THE POST–COLD WAR ERA

Reflections on Ted Robert Gurr

ONE OF THE MOST COMMON FORMS of revolution that has occurred since the late eighteenth century has been "nationalist" revolution to end foreign rule and establish a country's independence. Successful nationalist revolutions led to the independence from overseas colonial rule of the United States in the late eighteenth century, most Latin American countries in the 1820s, and numerous countries in the twentieth century, especially from the end of World War II to the collapse of the Portuguese empire in 1975.

From the perspective of the post–Cold War era, a discussion of nationalist revolution seems unnecessary since the great European colonial empires have been dismantled. Following Britain's turnover of Hong Kong to China in 1997, the few remaining European colonies are tiny in population and territory (mainly islands). More important, their inhabitants, for whatever reason, very much want colonial rule to continue.

Nevertheless, while European colonial rule has effectively ended, nationalist revolution remains a prominent feature of the post–Cold War era in the form of the many "secessionist" struggles that have continued despite the end of the Cold War, and the many new such conflicts that the end of the Cold War appears to have helped ignite, especially in the former Soviet Union and former Yugoslavia. These secessionist efforts have been launched primarily on behalf of ethnic or cultural groups that are a minority in an existing country, but that compose a majority in a specific region of that country. The government of the larger state almost always opposes these secessionist efforts. This can result in secessionist movements attempting to achieve their aims by violent, revolutionary means. (There are, of course, many relatively nonviolent secessionist movements, just as there were many relatively nonviolent anticolonial movements.)

But while movements seeking independence from overseas European colonial rule by violent means were generally regarded as revolutionary, movements seeking independence from geographically contiguous states have not been seen as such. Indeed, the term "secessionist" often has a negative connotation; those who seek it are often portrayed as pursuing narrow, divisive aims. Those who seek secession, however, do not see themselves in this light, but as nationalists instead.

It is not my purpose here to pass judgment on whether secessionist efforts (either in particular or in general) are "good" or "bad." Instead, I seek to explain how secessionist efforts can be understood as a form of nationalist revolution arising from causes similar to what Ted Robert Gurr argued was an important cause of revolution in general: relative deprivation. But while Gurr emphasized the economic aspect of relative deprivation as a cause of revolution, I will argue here that secessionist revolution (whether violent or nonviolent) results more from a sense of political relative deprivation, and that this sense of political relative deprivation has become especially heightened in the post–Cold War era. But before examining the specifics of relative deprivation in the post–Cold War era, it is first necessary to review how Gurr understood the concept.

GURR'S VIEW OF RELATIVE DEPRIVATION

In his book *Why Men Rebel* (1970), Gurr identified "relative deprivation" as the motive that could lead to revolution. Gurr defined relative deprivation as "a perceived discrepancy between men's value expectations and their value capabilities" (1970, 13)—value expectations being what people thought they were entitled to, and value capabilities being what they thought they could actually achieve in their circumstances. As Gurr put it, "Societal conditions that increase the average level or intensity of expectations without increasing capabilities increase the intensity of discontent" (1970, 13).

While not without its critics,[1] the relative deprivation concept is useful because it provides an explanation for the apparent paradox that revolution does not usually occur in the very poorest countries, but in ones that have achieved a certain degree of economic growth instead. Having no expectations that they could improve their miserable circumstances, people in the poorest countries have tended not to carry out revolutions. On the other hand, people whose circumstances are improving but whose expectations are growing at an even faster pace have become frustrated and have launched revolutions against regimes that could not or would not satisfy their desires. Gurr identified a period of "decline following a prolonged period of improvement" (1970, 101) as being especially likely to cause a sense of relative deprivation.

Gurr acknowledged that there could be several different types of relative deprivation, but regarded economic relative deprivation as being the most salient: "the intensity of relative deprivation is greatest with respect to discrepancy affecting economic values, less with respect to security and communality values, least with respect to participation, self-realization, status, or ideational coherence values" (1970, 361). In *Why Men Rebel*, then, Gurr did not see a sense of political relative deprivation as being a particularly strong motivating force leading to revolution.

POLITICAL RELATIVE DEPRIVATION

I argue, however, that in the conditions of the post–Cold War era, the demands of regionally dominant minorities for secession from multi-ethnic states are likely to increase. To understand why this is the case requires an understanding of the political aspects of relative deprivation, and its relative strength under both Cold War and post–Cold War conditions.

Let us consider a hypothetical country, X-istan (see Figure 1) with two ethnic groups: X and Y. In X-istan as a whole, the X's outnumber the Y's. But there is a region in X-istan, known as Y-istan, where the Y's outnumber the X's. Two assumptions will be made here:

Figure 1:

X-istan and Y-istan

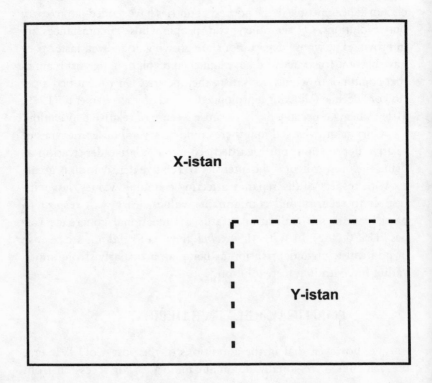

1. All other things being equal, it is highly likely that the X's would prefer (would vote for, even fight for) X-istan to remain intact and not permit Y-istan to secede.

There may be a number of reasons why preventing secession is preferable to the X's: Y-istan may contain valuable resources that the X's don't want to lose; the X's fear that X-istan will lose influence internationally if their country shrinks; the X's may fear that if Y-istan secedes, one or more other regions (A-, B-, and/or C-istan) may then also want to secede; or even that the secession of Y-istan will ultimately lead to X-istan's loss of independence. But while the reason, or combination of reasons, why the X's wish to prevent the Y's from seceding undoubtedly varies from case to case, the assumption appears unquestionably valid (at least through the end of the Cold War): the retreat of Western states from their colonies aside, virtually all governments have been unwilling to allow secession. Despite the voluntary breakup of the USSR in 1991, this continues to be true for most governments (including the 15 newly independent republics of the former Soviet Union) in the post–Cold War era. On the other hand:

2. All other things being equal, it is highly likely that the Y's would prefer (would vote for, and might even fight for) Y-istan to secede from X-istan.

The Y's might prefer this simply because they believe it is better to be the majority in a smaller country than a permanent minority in a larger one—especially if they are treated discriminatorily in that larger state.

The fact that there has not been much secession from geographically contiguous territory indicates that the validity of this assumption is open to serious question. But this lack of secession might be due to one of two different reasons. First, the regionally dominant minority might not want to secede. Where this is true, the assumption would be invalid. But second, the regionally dominant minority might want to secede, but is either prevented from doing so by force or fears that it will be so. In this case, the assumption would be valid.

This brings us to an important point. When it comes to secession, the desire of those who seek it alone does not decide whether it occurs. The role of force—whether applied, threatened, or implied—plays a crucial role. In the hypothetical case of X-istan, where the Y's want to secede but the X's do not want them to, it is likely that the X's will be able to prevent the Y's from seceding in any military contest over this issue.

Like all other countries, however, X-istan does not exist in a void, but in a system of international relations. While neither the X-istan government nor the Y-istan secessionist movement can much affect it, the existing system of international relations can significantly affect both the relative strength of the forces seeking and opposing secession as well as the prevailing norms and expectations in which they operate. Let us consider first how the Cold War system of international relations affected the forces seeking and opposing secession in X-istan, as well as some actual cases.

SECESSION AND THE COLD WAR SYSTEM OF INTERNATIONAL RELATIONS

X-istan may have come to rule over Y-istan through conquering it in the past. Or maybe the X's and the Y's were both conquered by a European power that drew artificial borders that included Y-istan within X-istan during the period of colonial rule that X-istan inherited upon independence. In neither case, however, did the Y's ever consent to being a permanent minority within X-istan.[2]

Although this situation usually came about through the use of force well before the onset of the Cold War, it was effectively maintained during it. If X-istan was a dictatorship, it maintained this situation through the use of force. On the other hand, if X-istan was a democracy, it sought to pacify the Y's through some degree of accommodation, but was unwilling to allow the Y's to vote on whether or not they wanted to secede, as described earlier.

But whether it was a dictatorship or democracy, the X-istan government was, during the Cold War, greatly aided in its efforts to prevent the secession of Y-istan by the policies of both superpowers. If X-istan were allied to the United States, Washington characteristically opposed secession from it for fear that the secessionists either were communists or might be allied to the Soviet Union. Even if the secessionists were "pro-Western," Washington did not wish to risk alienating an established ally in X-istan—or any other allied government facing a secessionist movement—through supporting a movement seeking secession from it.

Similarly, if X-istan were allied to the Soviet Union, Moscow characteristically opposed secession from it for fear that the secessionists either were or might be allied to the United States. Even if the secessionists were Marxist, Moscow did not wish to risk alienating an established ally in X-istan—or any other allied government facing a secessionist movement—through supporting a movement seeking secession from it. In retrospect, it appears that Moscow had an even greater incentive than Washington to oppose secessionism for fear of the precedent this would set for regionally dominant minorities in other Marxist states, including the USSR itself.

During the Cold War, then, the X-istan government was likely to receive military assistance from either the United States or the USSR in combating the Y-istan secessionist movement. On the other hand, the Y-istan secessionists were unlikely to receive any meaningful assistance from either superpower even if its rival was supporting the X-istan government. Thus, during the Cold War, the Y-istan secessionist movement was highly unlikely to achieve its aim. Indeed, the Cold War system of international relations was so biased against secession that the Y's themselves probably had little expectation of achieving it, and hence felt little incentive to join or give meaningful support to any Y-istan secessionist movement.

Although a hypothetical one, the case of X-istan was typical of the Cold War period. In general, neither the United States nor the Soviet Union supported secessionist efforts. On the few occasions when either of them did, this support was undertaken not to actually help a secessionist movement achieve its aim but to weaken the government it was fighting against. And such support was limited and temporary, being ended when a larger goal was achieved or a greater opportunity presented itself.[3]

The United States, for example, did back prerevolutionary Iran's support for Kurdish rebels in Iraq during the early 1970s. But once Iraq accepted Iranian terms with regard to delimiting the waterway that runs between them, Iranian—and American—support for the Kurds ceased (Helms 1984, 148–50). Similarly, Moscow gave some support to the Marxist guerrillas in Eritrea seeking secession from the pro-American government of Ethiopia. But after a Marxist revolution occurred in Ethiopia in 1974 that brought a pro-Soviet regime to power, Moscow ceased whatever support it had been giving the Eritrean Marxists and actually provided considerable military support to the Ethiopian Marxist effort to suppress the insurgency (Golan 1988, 278–9).

Secession was so difficult during the Cold War period that it only occurred on three occasions—all of which involved highly unusual circumstances. The first case was the withdrawal of Syria from the United Arab Republic in 1961. This was a highly unusual case since the creation of the United Arab Republic in 1958 involved the union of two independent and geographically discontiguous states—Egypt and Syria—under the leadership of Egypt's Jamal 'Abd al-Nasir. The Syrian Ba'th Party agreed to the merger partly because they needed Egyptian help in eliminating their communist rivals. Furthermore, it appears that the Syrian Ba'th leadership fully, albeit erroneously, expected that they—not the Egyptians—would dominate the UAR. Once their communist rivals were defeated and their illusions about dominating the UAR were shattered, the Syrian Ba'th Party reasserted Syria's independence by seceding from the UAR. And since Syria was geographically distant from Egypt, 'Abd al-Nasir was not in a position to defeat the Syrians militarily (Kerr 1971, 7–25).

The second case was the peaceful withdrawal of Singapore from the newly formed Malaysian Federation. This was an unusual case because Malaya, Singapore, and two colonies on North Borneo from which Malaysia was created had all been ruled separately by the British. They were joined together in 1961 in what was seen as an anticommunist measure. The predominantly Chinese citizenship and leadership of Singapore, however, soon found being a minority in a predominantly Muslim country to be unsatisfactory. More important, the Muslim leadership of Malaysia feared the potential political strength of the economically powerful Chinese in Singapore, and thus were happy to let Singapore secede in 1965 in order to preserve their own power in Malaysia as a whole (Andaya and Andaya 1982, 270–6).

The third case—Bangladesh—was also highly unusual, since the "region" that seceded from Pakistan was geographically discontiguous from the rest of the country. It was also unusual because an external power, India, intervened forcefully on behalf of the secessionists. And again unlike most other cases in which either the United States, the USSR, or sometimes both superpowers supported governments seeking to prevent secession, neither superpower was willing to provide significant military support to Pakistan in order to preserve the unity of that country. The United States—and China—formally backed the Pakistani position, but did nothing to help it once India intervened. The USSR, uncharacteristically, did support Bangladeshi secession, but more diplomatically than militarily. Further, it did so more as part of its larger policy of backing India than out of any interest in Bangladesh itself (Brown 1972, 222–5).

Bangladesh was unusual not only for being geographically discontiguous to the country it sought secession from, but also for having a strong external power intervene on behalf of the secessionists. Thus, Bangladesh did little to encourage secessionists who were seeking independence from a country that was geographically contiguous to their region and did not have a powerful external ally willing to intervene militarily on their behalf, but where the country it was trying to extricate itself from was receiving military support from one of the superpowers. These, of course, were the circumstances in which the overwhelming majority of secessionist movements found themselves.[4]

In general, then, the obstacles facing secessionist movements during the Cold War period were so great that it is hardly surprising that virtually all of them failed to achieve independence. In retrospect, what was surprising was that several secessionist movements fought for years or even decades despite all the obstacles they faced and the frustration of not being able to achieve their goal. Among the strongest and most persistent secessionist movements during the Cold War were the Eritreans (from Ethiopia), the southern Sudanese (from Sudan), the Tamils (from Sri Lanka), the Kurds (from Iraq, Iran, and Turkey), and the Moros (from the Philippines). Considering the obstacles faced by secessionists during the Cold War years, these secessionist movements clearly must have been very strongly motivated to fight so long and so fruitlessly. But while they did not achieve their ultimate aim during this period, they at least achieved the lesser aim of avoiding being defeated—a not inconsiderable accomplishment considering the hostile environment in which they operated.

SECESSION AND THE POST–COLD WAR SYSTEM OF INTERNATIONAL RELATIONS

Let us return to the hypothetical case of X-istan. In the post–Cold War era, it may well be that the Y's still want to secede from X-istan (indeed, as will be discussed later, the Y's may want this now more than ever). If a referendum were held in Y-istan alone, a strong vote in favor of independence for the region might be expected.

The government of X-istan, however, does not want to allow the Y's to secede. Furthermore, even if (perhaps especially if) X-istan is a newly democratizing state, a majority of X's do not want the Y's to secede. If the entire citizenry of X-istan were allowed to vote in a referendum on whether Y-istan should become independent, the motion would fail. Finally, since the X's outnumber the Y's, and since the X's control X-istan's military establishment, the X's are in a strong position to forcibly prevent Y-istan from seceding. In the post–Cold War era, then, the balance of forces inside X-istan does not favor the cause of Y-istan independence, just as was true during the Cold War era.

The system of international relations in the post–Cold War era, however, does not have the same strong bias against secessionist movements that it did during the Cold War era. There are three changes in particular that have served to reduce this bias. First, there is no longer a strong Soviet Union that X-istan can turn to for support. Post-Soviet Russia is not willing to provide X-istan with military assistance unless X-istan can pay for it with hard currency (which it probably cannot).

Second, with the demise of the Soviet Union, the United States is no longer concerned about the possibility that the independence of Y-istan will somehow redound to the benefit of Moscow or, there being none, any other global adversary. While Washington might not favor Y-istan independence, Congress and American public opinion are unwilling to provide massive military assistance to X-istan just so it can suppress the Y's.

Third, and most important, in just a very short period of time, the post–Cold War era has so far witnessed a massive amount of secession from geographically contiguous states. The demise of the USSR has given birth to 15 independent states. In addition, Yugoslavia has broken up into 5 states, and Czechoslovakia and Ethiopia into 2 states each.

Thus, while the Y-istan secessionists face significant opposition from the X-istan government, these changes in the post–Cold War system of international relations have led the Y's to draw two conclusions. First, the fact that so many other small nations have successfully seceded has convinced the Y's that the time is now more auspicious than ever to become independent. Second, the knowledge that neither the U.S. nor Russia is likely to provide X-istan with much help, if any, in suppressing the Y's has significant strategic implications.

During the Cold War, superpower support for the X-istan campaign to suppress the Y-istan secessionist movement meant that the X-istan government, and the X's as a whole, did not have to bear all the costs of this effort. The elimination or severe reduction of such external support during the post–Cold War era, though, means that the X-istan government must bear the entire cost of any effort to suppress the Y's. As a result, the Y's may calculate that while they cannot defeat the X's militarily, they can more easily wear them out if X-istan is not receiving external support.

If X-istani nationalism is strong among the X's, the X-istan government may still try to suppress Y-istani secession despite the absence of external support. But if the conflict becomes prolonged, the X's themselves might indeed become tired of bearing the human and financial costs that attempting to suppress the Y's entails. If X-istan is a democracy, the government may come to fear that the growing unpopularity of the war will cause it to be voted out of office. While previously unthinkable, allowing Y-istan to secede may come to be seen by X-ish public opinion and the X-istan government as much less worse than continuing the war.

Although not as typical as it was for the Cold War era, the case of X-istan described here is certainly not untypical for the post–Cold War era. In addition to those states that seceded from the USSR, Yugoslavia, Czechoslovakia, and Ethiopia that have been generally recognized internationally, secessionists have established de facto though as yet unrecognized independent states in Northern Somaliland, Chechnya, the Transdniester, and Abkhazia. Most of the longest-lived secessionist movements of the Cold War era (the Tamils, Kurds, Moros, and southern Sudanese) are still fighting— some of them harder than ever. Further, the post–Cold War era has witnessed the emergence of new, or renewed, secessionist movements in Xinjiang, Tibet, Kashmir, East Timor, Kosovo, other small Muslim nations in the Northern Caucasus besides the Chechens, and elsewhere.

Finally, certain longstanding Western democracies have witnessed the post–Cold War resurgence of regional nationalist movements, including those in Catalonia, northern Italy ("Padania"), Scotland, and Quebec. While not all regional nationalist movements are pursuing independence, some do seek independence through democratic means. Such a movement appears close to achieving this in Quebec, where in the last referendum those voting for independence lost by a very slender margin and where they can probably force another such referendum to be held, which they might just win (Doran 1996, 97–101).

One factor that has encouraged these movements is that the almost automatic opposition to secession that was characteristic of the Cold War system of international relations has been considerably relaxed in the new post–Cold War system—not just for X-istan, but in general. Indeed, far from opposing secession, the government of Russian President Boris Yeltsin has done much to encourage it through (1) Yeltsin's acquiescence to (even insistence upon) the breakup of the USSR at the end of 1991 into its 15 constituent "union republics," as they were known during the Soviet era (Matlock 1995, 633–8); (2) providing sufficient support to secessionist movements operating in some of those newly independent republics to the extent that they have achieved de facto secession from them (Transdniester from Moldova as well as Abkhazia from Georgia) (Crowther 1994; Slider 1997, 172); and (3) the withdrawal of Russian forces from and the de facto independence of Chechnya after the failure of a nearly two-year major Russian military effort to defeat secessionist forces there (Tolz 1996). Unlike the Soviet Union of the past, then, post-Soviet Russia has acted effectively to promote secession and ineffectively to suppress it.

While the United States has generally not done anything to promote secession in the post–Cold War era, it too has acted ineffectively to suppress it. Right through 1991, when nationalist forces calling for independence were gaining strength throughout the USSR, the Bush administration in vain hoped that the USSR would remain intact (Rosenthal 1991). Similarly, the Clinton administration's acquiescence to Russian military intervention in Chechnya obviously did little to persuade the Chechens to abandon their cause (Blank 1996, 20–5). While the United States has generally not been willing to militarily support specific instances of secession the way Russia has in Transdniester and Abkhazia, Washington has been unwilling to act forcefully to prevent it either.[5]

Besides the reduction of Moscow's and Washington's ability or willingness to prevent secession from other countries, the post Cold War has also witnessed an increased demand for it. In order to understand this, we must return to our discussion of relative deprivation.

POLITICAL RELATIVE DEPRIVATION IN THE POST–COLD WAR ERA

Although Gurr de-emphasized the importance of political relative deprivation, he did cite examples of how expectations can be

quickly raised "with respect to power values" through the demonstration effect. He wrote that, "Ghana's attainment of independence
in 1957 intensified expectations of political independence among
African leaders throughout the continent" (1970, 97).

This example is instructive. People in other sub-Saharan African
colonies had wanted independence before Ghana achieved it. They
were also aware that other European colonies were becoming independent in Asia, the Middle East, and even North Africa. The effect
of Ghana's independence on the rest of sub-Saharan Africa, though,
was electric: if black Africans could achieve independence in Ghana,
it is not difficult to understand why black Africans elsewhere felt
they not only should, but could become independent as well. Just as
important, the fact that Britain was willing to grant independence to
Ghana suggested that it would grant independence to its other sub-
Saharan African colonies (which it soon did). Further, if Britain—
the strongest and richest of the European colonial powers—could
withdraw from its colonies, this suggested that the other European
colonial powers that were not as strong or as rich could leave too.
All of them eventually did, of course. Ironically, though, the poorest
and weakest European colonial power in Africa—Portugal—resisted
this logic the longest and only succumbed to it after the effort to
keep its colonies led to a revolution in Portugal itself.

It is possible to argue with Gurr over this example. Was Ghana's
independence alone responsible for escalating demands for independence elsewhere in sub-Saharan Africa, or did the independence of
India, Indonesia, North Vietnam and other Third World colonies
outside of sub-Saharan Africa contribute to them? The Ghanaians,
arguably, were inspired by one or more of these successful independence movements outside of sub-Saharan Africa.[6]

But whether Ghanaian independence served as the primary or
only an incremental example for African independence movements
is less relevant than the fact that (unlike secessionist movements during the Cold War era but very much, as I argue, like such movements
during the post–Cold War era) the structure of the Cold War system
of international relations militated against the continuation of overseas European colonial rule. Africans had sought to throw off European colonial rule before the Cold War but had been unable to do

so. Under the changed circumstances of the Cold War era—especially the decline in power of the European colonial states that resulted from World War II—Africans, and others, saw that they had an increased opportunity to bring about their long sought goal of independence, and this increased opportunity led to an increased demand for it.

Has the breakup of the USSR served to galvanize secessionists in other countries in a way similar to Gurr's description of how the independence of Ghana affected the rest of sub-Saharan Africa? Some might point out that the breakup of the USSR occurred under highly unusual circumstances not present elsewhere. The leadership of several of the republics that became independent—especially those in Central Asia—did not seek independence but had it thrust upon them by Yeltsin in December 1991 (Garthoff 1994, 485). There are very few leaders like Yeltsin willing to allow—or more accurately, insist—that regionally dominant minorities become independent whether they have demanded to or not.

Indeed, it appears in retrospect that Yeltsin did not engineer the breakup of the USSR in 1991 out of any profound belief in the right of secession. Instead, he appears to have done this more for the short-term aim of depriving the last Soviet leader, Mikhail Gorbachev, of a government to lead (Matlock 1995, 654–5). Russia's secession from the USSR also resulted in elevating the Russian presidency from a subordinate position vis-à-vis Gorbachev to the most powerful post in the former Soviet Union. There are signs that Yeltsin anticipated that the independence of the non-Russian republics would only be nominal, and that they would very much remain under Russian influence (Petro and Rubinstein 1997, 115). Popular support for political parties calling for the restoration of the USSR indicates that significant elements within the Russian public have not reconciled themselves to Russia's diminished territory and stature in the world (White et al. 1997, 123, 224–5). (In other words, their preferences are consistent with those of the X's of X-istan who do not wish to see the Y's secede.)

Some might argue, then, that to the extent that some of the former Soviet republics did not seek independence but attained it

anyway, that the Yeltsin leadership did not intend for Russian influence over the non-Russian republics to end (or perhaps even to
decline) as a result of the breakup of the USSR, and that there are
powerful forces within Russia that seek to reconstitute it, the
breakup of the USSR occurred under highly unusual circumstances
that are not present in other countries. Thus, secessionist movements in other countries cannot derive encouragement from the
breakup of the USSR in the same way that independence movements elsewhere derived encouragement from British withdrawal
from India or Ghana.

This argument, however, is flawed both in terms of the context
of the former USSR as well as in terms of how the breakup of this
state has affected secessionist movements in general. There are three
points to be made with regard to the ease with which the breakup
of the USSR could be reversed. First, while it is true that the communist leaders of the Central Asian republics in particular did not
seek independence, nationalist movements had risen up in some of
them (Dawisha and Parrott 1994, 80–6). Kazakhstan's Nazarbayev
particularly sought to avoid the breakup of the USSR (Garthoff
1994, 485). It must be remembered, though, that it was in Kazakhstan in December 1986 where large-scale non-Russian nationalist
forces first manifested themselves during the Gorbachev period (Nahaylo and Swoboda 1990, 255–8). Nazarbayev and other Central
Asian communist leaders may not have actively sought independence due to their fear of the strength of these nationalist forces.
Once their countries became independent, however, the communist
leaders of the three wealthiest and most important Central Asian
states—Kazakhstan, Uzbekistan, and Turkmenistan—have managed
to keep the nationalist opposition in check and even to successfully
claim the nationalist mantle for themselves. Thus, while they may
have feared that independence would spell the end of their political
careers back in 1990–91, they would not now voluntarily give it up
after having successfully made the transition to—and acquired the
prestige of—being the rulers of independent states (Beddoes 1998,
S16–S17).

Second, Yeltsin's acquiescence to the breakup of the USSR was
not made purely for the sake of getting rid of Gorbachev and pro-

moting himself. Secessionist sentiment had grown especially strong in the Baltic republics, Ukraine, Moldova, and the South Caucasus. While Gorbachev was determined to keep the USSR intact, Yeltsin "concluded there was no future in negotiating a new union" and so agreed to its dissolution (White *et al.* 1997, 39).

Third, it is true that after disappointment with Yeltsin's initial economic liberalization measures set in, communist and national-ist parties advocating the reconstitution of the USSR gained popu-lar support. Further, their resurgence pushed Yeltsin into a more Russian nationalist direction also, leading him to launch his disas-trous military effort to prevent Chechnya from seceding from the Russian Federation. Yet as Russian public opinion turned against the war in Chechnya, the leaders of these communist and nation-alist parties distanced themselves from the war effort (White *et al.* 1997, 249). For they understood that while their constituents would like to see the restoration of the USSR, these same con-stituents are not prepared to pay a high price to achieve this goal or even the far more modest goal of keeping the Russian Federa-tion intact.

Post–Soviet Russia, then, does seem to resemble the hypotheti-cal case of post–Cold War X-istan discussed earlier: Russian (X-istani) nationalism is strong, but when the conflict to suppress Chechen (Y-istani) secessionism became prolonged, the Russians (X's) themselves became tired of bearing the human and financial costs that attempting to suppress the Chechens (Y's) entailed. And since Russia (X-istan) is democratizing—if not fully a democracy—the Yeltsin government came to fear that the growing unpopularity of the war would cause it to be voted out of office in 1996. Thus, while unthinkable previously, permitting de facto Chechen (Y-istani) secession came to be seen by Russian (X-ish) public opinion and the Yeltsin (X-istan) government as much less worse than con-tinuing the war.

The Soviet Union, though, did not resemble X-istan in one cru-cial respect. Instead of being just an ordinary country, it was one of the superpowers that acted to prevent secession during the Cold War era. The fact that this state in particular broke apart has had a profound affect on secessionist movements elsewhere.

The breakup of the USSR has directly inspired other previously inactive or even nonexistent secessionist movements in or near the former Soviet Union. There were, for example, no active Chechen, Abkhaz, or Transdniestrian secessionist movements before this event. The fact that only the union republics of the former USSR became independent created a sense of political relative deprivation among these other groups.[7] The secessionists of Abkhazia and Transdniester appear to have reasoned that if Georgia and Moldova could secede from the USSR, then their regions could secede from Georgia and Moldova (Crowther 1994; Slider 1997). And for the Chechens, the independence of so many other nations from Moscow's control (and perhaps even Russian support for secessionists in Abkhazia and the Transdniester) only inflamed their long-standing desire to free themselves from Russian rule (Tolz 1996).

Similarly, although there had been some Uighur opposition to Chinese rule in Xinjiang in the first part of the twentieth century, this movement was relatively moribund after being crushed at the end of World War II. Secessionist nationalism flared up again in Xinjiang, however, after the independence of the states of former Soviet Central Asia. What is remarkable about this movement in Xinjiang is that it has flared up despite receiving virtually no support or even encouragement from the newly independent Central Asian republics that do not want to antagonize China. For the Uighurs, it also appears to be a sense of political relative deprivation that has inspired them: if their Turkic cousins across the border could become independent from Moscow, perhaps they too can become independent from China (Gladney 1997, 287–8).

In addition, the breakup of the USSR has affected secessionist movements throughout the world. For if the Soviet Union—a military superpower—could not or would not prevent secession by its regionally dominant minorities, how can a less powerful government long resist similar demands? For any group looking for a reason to be optimistic about the prospects for their particular region to secede and become independent, the breakup of the USSR has surely provided it.[8] The successful secession of Slovakia, Slovenia, Croatia, Macedonia, and Eritrea can only underline this conclusion. And while Bosnia's secession from Yugoslavia has obviously been highly problematic, secessionist movements can even take heart from it. Bosnia was a case in which NATO forces eventually intervened on behalf of the secessionists even if this was done for humanitarian reasons and not out of support for the principle of secession in general or for Bosnian secession in particular.

MOTIVATIONS FOR OPPOSING SECESSION

Despite the increased demand for secession that appears to have resulted from the breakup of the USSR as well as the distinctive features of the post–Cold War system of international relations that have reduced the obstacles to its achievement, it is not predestined that many more—perhaps even any more—secessionist movements will achieve independence for their regions. For whatever else may have changed, there is still the basic fact that not only are almost all X-istans unwilling to allow their Y-istans to secede, but also that, even without external assistance, the X-istans possess considerable military capacities to prevent secession.

This being the case, some might argue that most secessionist movements have little better opportunity to attain independence in the post–Cold War era than they did in the Cold War era. The states that have experienced secession are all former Marxist regimes. Their breakup owes more to the collapse of communism than anything else. Secession from these states, then, is of little relevance to more "normal" states that are as willing and able to prevent secession now as they were previously.

But even if, as has been argued here, the transition from the Cold War system of international relations (which acted to prevent secession) to the post–Cold War one (which is more permissive of it) affects all countries, this does not mean that governments facing secessionist movements will cease to oppose them. All that is being said here is that the successful secession that has occurred from the USSR and other countries so far in the post–Cold War era has encouraged secessionist movements elsewhere while the transition to the post–Cold War system of international relations has meant that governments opposing secessionist movements are far less likely to receive external military assistance than they were during the Cold War.

This being the case, governments opposing secession have a choice: (1) they can decide to grant independence to secessionist movements in order to avoid (or further avoid) the high human, financial, and domestic political costs of attempting to suppress them that could well continue indefinitely; or (2) they can decide to deny independence to secessionist movements despite their inability to suppress them or to avoid the high costs that must be borne so long as the effort to suppress them continues.

The argument presented here suggests that if states were rational, those facing high cost, long-term efforts to suppress secessionist movements would make the first choice. For if such efforts are unlikely to succeed anyway, then X-istan may as well just give in to the Y-istani secessionists and thereby avoid the high costs of fruitlessly trying to suppress them.

The fact that so many governments appear to have made the second choice does not prove that the argument presented here is wrong. Nor does it prove that states making this choice are irrational. There are two other possibilities. First, governments that choose to suppress secessionists may initially convince themselves that doing so will only involve a low-cost, short-term effort (the Yeltsin government, for example, convinced itself that Grozny, the Chechen capital, "would be captured in a matter of hours" when the Russian military intervention against it was first launched) (Tolz 1996, 318). Second, and more important, a government might decide to continue fighting against a secessionist movement that it has failed to defeat after many years or even decades of fighting, with the full understanding that this very costly effort is unlikely to succeed in the future either. Such a government is willing to continue this high-cost, long-term counterinsurgency effort, which it probably cannot win, because *it is more fearful of what will happen if it gives in to the secessionist movement* even though this will bring to an end the high cost of attempting to suppress it.

If the government of X-istan is a dictatorship, allowing Y-istan to secede could be extremely dangerous. For if the Y's can escape from X-istani dictatorial rule, the X's themselves may see a greater opportunity to escape from it also—not through secession, but through overthrowing the regime. The communist government of China, then, may feel motivated to cling tenaciously to both Xinjiang and Tibet for fear that letting them go would demonstrate that it is weak, thus leading to the rise of opposition within the Chinese population. Similarly, the Islamic fundamentalist regime in Sudan undoubtedly continues its fruitless effort to subdue non-Muslim secessionist forces in the southern part of the country for fear that allowing the south to secede would stimulate opposition to it in the Muslim north.

Democratic governments can certainly do more to accommodate regionally dominant minorities in order to dissuade, not prevent, them from seceding. And to a much greater extent than dictatorial regimes, democratic governments may ultimately be able to accept secession, shrug it off, and carry on, as the Czechs did with regard to Slovakia, the Russians with the non-Russian union republics of the former USSR (at least so far), and Canada would undoubtedly do after the secession of Quebec. There is one set of circumstances, however, in which even democratic governments will undertake a high-cost, long-term counterinsurgency effort to prevent secession: when the secession of one region of the country can be expected to stimulate secessionist movements in several other parts of it.

An important reason why predominantly Hindu India has fought so hard to keep hold of predominantly Muslim Kashmir is the demonstration effect Kashmir's secession could be expected to have on regionally dominant minorities elsewhere in India, including the Sikhs of Punjab, various ethnic groups in the northeast, and possibly the Tamils in the south, and others. Many Hindus, then, fear that the secession of Kashmir would set a precedent for other ethnic groups to seek secession as well (Carley 1997, 7).

Similar considerations appear to explain the irony of Boris Yeltsin's virtual insistence that the 14 non-Russian republics of the former USSR become independent in 1991 on the one hand and his 1994–96 military effort to keep tiny Chechnya inside Russia. The independence of the non-Russian union republics in 1991 was not seen as threatening the territorial integrity of the Russian

Federation, especially since the Yeltsin government appears to have mistakenly thought that these newly independent republics would remain firmly under Russian influence anyway. By contrast, the Yeltsin government feared that the secession of Chechnya would ultimately lead to the secession of other "autonomous republics" from Russia (Blank 1996, 11–12).

As India has shown, a democracy can successfully pursue a protracted counterinsurgency effort to prevent the secession of a region. Doing this, however, creates two problems. First, if a democratic government acts forcefully to prevent a region from deciding democratically whether to secede, then democracy is obviously not operative in that region. Second, a protracted military effort by a democratic government to prevent a recalcitrant region from seceding may ultimately undermine democracy in the country as a whole if it leads to the rise of virulently nationalist parties. The Russian withdrawal from Chechnya in 1996 showed that the Yeltsin government ultimately valued democracy more than unity. By contrast, the increasingly powerful Hindu nationalist forces in India appear to value unity more than democracy (Juergensmeyer 1993, 81–90). Ironically, then, while a protracted unsuccessful military effort to defeat a secessionist movement can undermine a dictatorship, it can also undermine a democracy.

This analysis would suggest that the states that would most vigorously oppose secession are dictatorships facing secessionist movements in several regions of the country. The success of even one secessionist movement in such a situation could lead to the unraveling of both the regime and the country. Thus, it is not surprising that the Indonesian dictatorship, for example, has fiercely suppressed the secessionist movements that have risen up in many regions of that country (Kristoff 1998).

This analysis would also suggest that the states that would least vigorously oppose secession are democracies facing a secessionist movement in only one region of the country. The secession of this one region would leave behind a relatively cohesive nation that would not be subject to further secessionism. The prime example of this was when the Czechs readily consented to the division of Czechoslovakia into Czech and Slovak republics.

There are, however, some examples of democracies resorting to force to prevent just one region of a country from seceding. But where this occurs, it is usually the case that the "democratic" government is incompletely democratic, as with the Turkish government fighting against Kurdish secessionists (Barkey and Fuller 1997).

Gurr pointed out in his later work that if a democratic government takes action to accommodate it, a regionally dominant minority will not support violent secessionist movements but will settle for "autonomy" within the existing state (1993, 137). Indeed, this status might allow a regionally dominant minority to exercise political leverage over the majority for an extended period of time that would not be possible if it gained independence. For so long as it remains part of the existing state, a regionally dominant minority can selectively ally with contending factions from the majority group as well as hold out the threat of secession in order to extract additional benefits for itself from the larger state.

This, of course, is a game that can no longer be played once secession occurs. On the other hand, the cost of accommodating a regionally dominant minority may eventually appear more undesirable to the rest of the country than granting the minority independence. In other words, the majority may conclude it is better off without the minority. This appears to have been the Czech attitude toward Slovak secession (Svec 1992). It would be ironic indeed if the costs of accommodating a disgruntled regionally dominant minority within a democratic state eventually led to, in our hypothetical case, the X-istan government welcoming Y-istani secession instead of resisting it.

CONCLUSION

Looking back upon the revolutions of the twentieth century, what emerges is that those that had ambitious goals of transforming their societies in accordance with some nondemocratic utopian vision, and exporting this vision to other countries, all eventually failed or appear to be in the process of failing (Katz 1997). By contrast, an enduring achievement of twentieth-century revolutions, particularly in the Third World, has been the far more modest task of transforming so many colonies into independent states. Some of these independence movements fought so fiercely and tenaciously that they eventually convinced the European powers that the cost of continuing their colonial rule far outweighed any possible benefit of doing so. The independence of those colonies that struggled so tenaciously to achieve it had two results: (1) raising expectations in other colonies that they too could become independent; and (2) convincing the European powers that it was not worth the effort to retain colonial rule not just over those colonies that actively struggled for their independence, but also over any colonies where this even threatened to occur—which, of course, was most of them. These anticolonial revolutions, then, did not just affect the countries they were fought in, but established an international norm—showing absolutely no sign of weakening—against overseas European colonial rule where the inhabitants oppose it. These anticolonial revolutions, then, transformed not just the countries they were fought in, but international relations as a whole.

Similarly, the massive wave of secession that occurred in the wake of the collapse of communism has clearly fueled demands for secession elsewhere. It is not yet clear how much their efforts will convince other governments that the costs of preventing secession outweigh the benefits. I have argued here that governments attempting to prevent secession are far less likely to be able to share the costs of doing so with the major powers in the post–Cold War era than during the Cold War. This will only make preventing secession more difficult, hence increasing the sense of political relative deprivation that will spur demand for it. And the more it does occur, the more likely it is that an international norm will arise that secession cannot and should not be prevented where the inhabitants want it.

This is not to say that this will be "good." Although the breakup of the USSR and Czechoslovakia occurred peacefully, the breakup of Yugoslavia demonstrates that secession can lead to intense conflict. But so can the effort to prevent secession, as is currently being demonstrated in Kashmir, Xinjiang, the Tamil regions of Sri Lanka, southern Sudan, several parts of the former Soviet Union, and elsewhere.

Secession will not prove to be a panacea for resolving the problems of those who seek it, just as independence did not resolve—indeed, it often exacerbated—the problems of many former colonies. This warning, however, will not halt the demand for independence through secession, just as it did not stop the demand for independence through decolonization. And as the wave of decolonization did earlier, an expanding wave of secession will revolutionize international relations more profoundly and more permanently than more ambitious revolutionary programs that either have already proven themselves to be bankrupt or are in the process of doing so.

PART III

DEMOCRACY AND REVOLUTION

CHAPTER 5

DEMOCRACY, REVOLUTION, AND THE FUTURE

Reflections on Goodwin vs. Selbin

AT THE 1998 ANNUAL CONVENTION of the International Studies Association (ISA), both Jeff Goodwin and Eric Selbin presented papers discussing the potential for revolution in the post–Cold War era. Goodwin's paper argued that the "age of revolution" was essentially over, while Selbin's maintained that the potential for revolution in the post–Cold War era remained the "same as it ever was."

In his paper, Goodwin stated, *"No popular revolutionary movement . . . has ever overthrown a consolidated democratic regime"* (emphasis in original). He observed that during the Cold War, revolutions overthrew colonial regimes, personalist dictatorships, and at the end of the Cold War, Soviet-inspired communist regimes, but that "none overthrew a regime that even remotely resembled a democracy." He noted that during the interwar years, "Rightist movements did destroy democratic regimes in Germany, Italy, and Spain, but those regimes were of relatively recent vintage" (Goodwin 1998, 6). These regimes, in other words, were not consolidated democracies.

Regarding the post–Cold War era, Goodwin argued that the "seed bed for revolution is virtually desiccated:" colonialism has essentially ended, Moscow no longer dominates Eastern Europe, and "U.S. hegemony" over the Third World is "increasingly challenged." More importantly, "a transnational 'wave' of democratization has swept across large parts of East Asia, Eastern Europe, Latin America, and (to a lesser extent) Africa" (Goodwin 1998, 5).

As a result, he argued, "the coming decades are unlikely to exhibit the same scale of revolutionary conflict as the Cold War era precisely because of this vast political transformation." For whatever its causes, democracy has "counterrevolutionary consequences" (Goodwin 1998, 6). This is not because democracy eliminates social conflict. Indeed, democracy "encourages a veritable flowering of social conflict by providing the 'political space' or 'political opportunities' with which those groups outside ruling circles can make claims on political authorities and economic elites" (Goodwin 1998, 7).

Revolution, then, is a last, desperate resort that politically and economically deprived groups turn to when an undemocratic government refuses to address their demands, or to allow their expression. By allowing such groups both to express their demands and to seek satisfaction of them through the political process, democracy eliminates the incentive for embarking on the difficult and dangerous path of revolution. Those countries in which democracy becomes established, then, are those least likely to experience revolution. And at a time when democratization is spreading to so many countries, this leaves fewer and fewer nondemocracies available to be overthrown by revolution.

Selbin, by contrast, argued that "as global gaps between the haves and the have-nots increase and neo-liberalism fails to deliver on its promise, revolution will be more likely" (Selbin 1998, 2). Focusing primarily on Latin America, he noted that guerrilla movements are now operating in Bolivia, Colombia, Mexico, and Peru. He observed that while democracy has spread widely throughout Latin America, "even a cursory examination of the state of the hemisphere shows that meaningful democratic practices remain weak. Few of these democracies are inclusive, based instead on elite pacts and the continued marginalization of the region's indigenous population" (Selbin 1998, 6). He also noted that there have been several coups or near coups, as in Peru, Haiti, Venezuela, Paraguay, and Ecuador. Although supposedly democratic, the military still plays a large—even decisive—political role in many Latin American states (Selbin 1998, 6–7).

As has been widely observed, Latin America has also been undergoing a dramatic capitalist transformation. But Selbin argues that "the increasingly less than democratic procedures used to implement 'neo-liberal reforms' have done little or nothing to promote the social welfare of profoundly impoverished populations. More people in Latin America and the Caribbean live in poverty today than did twenty years ago" (Selbin 1998, 6). Latin America's supposedly increased democratization has not allowed its population to prevent this from happening.

As so many Latin Americans have not been able to satisfy their political and economic demands through the region's vaunted democratization, they have abundant incentive to seek their satisfaction through revolution. Selbin also notes that revolution has been a political tradition in Latin America for "at least 500 years" (Selbin 1998, 13). Revolution, then, is a long-established part of Latin American political culture. Selbin further observes that "the people of Latin America and the Caribbean will create their future with the tool-kit their culture provides them and revolution remains a ready tool" (Selbin 1998, 8).

These two arguments appear to be diametrically opposed to each other. If one is right, it would seem, then the other must necessarily be wrong. The question, then, is which is it: Is the age of revolution over are not?

Since Goodwin and Selbin are arguing about the future, their debate obviously will not finally be resolved until the future has arrived—and maybe not even then. Instead of attempting to definitively answer the question of whether or not the age of revolution is over, I seek to show how approaching this question with different assumptions can point to different answers to it. While there are clearly many factors involved, one of the most important for examining the likelihood of revolution in the post–Cold War era in particular is the relationship between democracy and revolution. It is around two different views of this relationship that I will structure this discussion of the future of revolution in the post–Cold War era.

Although Goodwin and Selbin disagree over whether there will be much revolution in the post–Cold War era, they both agree that democracy and revolution are inversely related. The more democratic a state is, the less susceptible it is to revolution. The less democratic a state is, the more susceptible it is to revolution. What they disagree about is just how democratic the world's democracies— especially the newer ones—actually are. Goodwin's view that democracy has been securely established in most (though not all) of the world is the basis for his prediction that the age of revolution is over. By contrast, Selbin's view that democracy has not been securely established, particularly in Latin America and other regions where it has only arrived recently, is the basis for his prediction that revolutions will continue to occur.

Furthermore, these are aggregate views. Goodwin readily concedes—indeed, he insists—that revolution is possible in countries that are not democratic. Similarly, Selbin is not predicting that revolution is likely in countries where democracy has long, deep roots; he argues instead that it is likely in countries where democracy has short, shallow roots. Leaving aside the Western democracies where neither Goodwin nor Selbin expects revolution on the one hand, and the nondemocracies where both expect revolution (or at least its attempt) on the other, the debate between Goodwin and Selbin focuses primarily on incompletely democratic or newly democratizing states such as those in Eastern Europe and the former Soviet Union, Latin America, Asia, and Africa.

Assuming, as Goodwin and Selbin do, that democracy and revolution are inversely related, then the character and extent of the democratization that has occurred in these incompletely democratic and newly democratizing states clearly has a large impact on their propensity for revolution. How meaningful, then, has democratization been in these countries? Has it developed sufficiently in them to forestall revolution or not?

Since democratization has not developed uniformly in all countries, answering these questions would require an individual assessment of each country experiencing it. This will not be undertaken here primarily since I do not wish to detract from my overall argument by engaging in a multitude of debates about particular cases. Even specialists on individual countries that are undergoing democratization often disagree on whether or to what extent the process is succeeding.

Nevertheless, a few general observations are in order. Selbin raised a serious question about the meaningfulness of democracy in those Latin American countries whose politics and economics are controlled by a European elite to the exclusion of the indigenous and mestizo population (1998). The meaningfulness of democracy is very much open to question in Russia, where politics and the economy appear to be dominated by a small elite and where both parliament and the political parties represented in it are extremely weak (Yavlinsky 1998). Although often vaunted as the "world's most populous democracy," India has witnessed the decline of its once dominant secular, inclusive political party and the rise of a religious nationalist, exclusive one (Cooper 1998). Fareed Zakaria has pointed to the prevalence of "illiberal democracies," which he sees as being considerably less peaceable or stable than true liberal democracies (1997). I argue elsewhere that ethnic groups dominant in a particular region of a country but that constitute a minority in the country as a whole often regard the prospect of being the majority in a smaller country as superior to being the minority in a larger one, even if the latter is democratic (chapter 4).

All this being said, however, Goodwin provides a persuasive argument as to why even incompletely democratic governments are less prone to revolution than dictatorships:

> democracy "translates" and channels a variety of social conflicts . . .
> into party competition for votes and the lobbying of representatives
> by "interest groups." Of course, this "translation" has sometimes
> taken violent forms, especially when and where the fairness of elec-
> toral contests is widely questioned. But the temptation to rebel
> against the state—which is rarely seized without trepidation under

any circumstances, given its life-or-death consequences—is generally quelled under democratic regimes by the knowledge that new
elections are but a few years off—and with them the chance to pun-
ish incumbent rulers. (Goodwin 1998, 6)

In other words, so long as the electoral process is perceived as
fair, opposition groups would prefer to participate in elections
rather than attempt revolution. Indeed, opposition groups may even
prefer to contest unfair elections rather than revolt if they believe
that, through a combination of internal and external pressure, subsequent elections will be fairer. This appears to have been the moti-
vation of Cuauhtemoc Cardenas who, after being declared the loser
in the Mexican presidential elections of 1988 that he—and many
others—believed he had won, continued to participate in the electoral process. And in fact, subsequent Mexican elections have become fairer: while the long-ruling Institutional Revolutionary Party
(PRI) still controls the presidency, opposition parties won a majority of seats in the Mexican Congress, and Cardenas himself was
elected mayor of Mexico City in 1997 (Dresser 1998).

This example points to the difficulty of determining how democratic a state is. For the determination must not only take into account the actual degree of fairness of the most recent or upcoming
elections, but also of expectations—those of opposition leaders as
well as the public in general—about the prospects for improved (or
continued) electoral fairness in the future. And of course, free elections alone do not make a democracy. There are a host of other factors affecting the opposition's willingness to participate in an
incomplete democracy—such as the extent to which it can express
its viewpoint in parliament and the press as well as the extent to
which it is free to organize in order to more effectively compete in
the next elections.

Democracy, then, is not something that is either fully present or
completely absent in many countries. What may influence opposition groups in those states in between is their expectations about
whether, through their participation, their particular polity can be
moved from a lesser to a greater degree of democratization. On the
other hand, fear that an electorally victorious opposition party will

destroy democracy and rule dictatorially once in power may induce
(or be used as an excuse) for the armed forces to preemptively can-
cel elections (as occurred in Algeria), or force the party they fear out
of office (as occurred in Turkey), resulting in their polities moving
from a greater to a lesser degree of democratization, or back to out-
right dictatorship (Layachi 1994; Yayla 1997). Assuming revolution
and democracy are inversely related, such actions may well increase
the prospects for revolution, which governments undertaking them
presumably seek to avoid.

In attempting to determine whether the age of revolution is
over, though, each individual country's day-to-day progress toward
or regression from democratization is less important than the degree
of long-term progress toward democracy that is being made in each
region as well as globally. For not only does this affect the countries
undergoing democratization, but it can have an impact on others as
well. For example, the spread of democracy generally in Latin
America during the 1980s may have served to delegitimize and undermine nondemocratic governments more effectively than when
autocratic regimes were the norm in the region previously.

As many have pointed out, modern democracy has only existed
for just over two centuries anywhere, and its spread to most countries has occurred only in the past few decades. Being of such recent
historical vintage, its permanency cannot be regarded as an empiri-
cally established fact—especially in those countries where it has only
recently developed.

Just how permanent is this recent wave of democratization? There
are essentially two views with regard to how progress toward
democracy on a worldwide basis has been and will continue to be
made. One maintains that this occurs on a linear basis, while the
other argues that it occurs on a cyclical one.

The argument for linear progress toward democracy was set
forth with great fanfare by Francis Fukuyama in *The End of History
and the Last Man* (1992). Fukuyama maintained that beyond the
desire for survival and for material well being, there is a basic
human desire for recognition by others as an equal (1992, 143–52).
Fukuyama sees this as the primordial force resulting in democracy,

since no other system of government allows this desire to be pursued, if not always satisfied, on a general basis (1992, 199–208). As a result of Marxism-Leninism and other nondemocratic ideologies having proved themselves inferior—especially to those living under them—to liberal democracy in this regard, the demand for liberal democracy has become increasingly universal (1992, 23–51). Thus, whether quickly or slowly, all countries not currently enjoying it are in the process of democratic transformation since nothing else can ultimately satisfy their citizens. While setbacks in any given country may occur, these are merely temporary glitches in the inexorable and ultimately irreversible linear progress toward democracy being made in all countries (1992, 211–22, 266–75).

The argument that democracy expands and contracts cyclically was made by Samuel Huntington in *The Third Wave* (1991). In this book, he maintained that the spread of democracy has occurred in three great "waves:" 1828–1926, 1943–1962, and 1974–1991. The first two waves, however, were followed by "reverse waves" (1922–42, and 1958–1975) in which some but not all of those states that had become democratic in the previous wave reverted to authoritarianism (1991, 13–26). In an article that appeared subsequent to the publication of this book, Huntington indicated that the "third wave" of democratization had ended and a third "reverse wave" had begun. As he put it, though, "With third-wave democracies, the problem is not overthrow but erosion: the intermittent or gradual weakening of democracy by those elected to lead it" (1996, 8).

While Huntington, at least in this book, did not see any permanent obstacles—cultural or otherwise—to the spread of democracy (1991, 310–11), he observed that it did not always survive, especially where it was relatively new and the problems it faced were overwhelming (290–4). While he did not predict that it would necessarily spread to all countries, Huntington did see the sphere of democracy steadily expanding through this wave process since fewer countries regressed from democracy to authoritarianism in the reverse waves than had advanced from authoritarianism to democracy in the preceding democratic waves. Further, while he saw countries with young democracies as most susceptible to reverse waves, he saw them as better candidates for successful democratization in the next democratic wave than countries with no previous history of democracy attempting it for the first time (1991, 295–6). Yet while Huntington expected countries that lost their democratic form of government to ultimately regain it, he implied that no democracy—not even a long-standing one—can be said to be completely immune to being overcome by the forces of authoritarianism, even if only temporarily. For him, the regular recurrence of reverse waves indicated that this process was inevitable.

In my view, it is impossible to determine at present whether democracy is spreading in a linear fashion or whether it expands and contracts cyclically. A considerable period of time may need to pass before either of these hypotheses can be definitively falsified. What is important to note about them here is that, assuming democracy and revolution are inversely related, each hypothesis has very different implications concerning whether the age of revolution is over. If democracy is indeed spreading inevitably throughout the world in a linear fashion, this would indicate that the prospects for revolution must necessarily diminish as a result. But if democracy expands and contracts cyclically, then the nondemocracies that periodically overthrow democracies are likely to become the targets of revolution.

Thus, the hypothesis that democracy is spreading in a linear fashion supports Goodwin's view that the age of revolution is over, while the hypothesis that democracy expands and contracts cyclically supports Selbin's view that it is not, assuming that democracy and revolution are inversely related.

But are democracy and revolution inversely related? Goodwin in particular appears to rule out the probability (if not the possibility) that there can be revolution against a democratic government. Selbin does not rule this out, but since he argues that the "democratizing" governments against which revolutionaries are active in Latin America are not really democratic, the possibility of revolution against a truly democratic government is not something he actually examines.

Goodwin, though, appears to admit the possibility that revolution can occur against newly democratizing governments. Thus, he explained the successful fascist revolutions against democratic governments in Germany, Italy, and Spain by noting that "those regimes were of relatively recent vintage" (1998, 6).

The circumstances leading to the downfall of democracy in Germany, Italy, and Spain were highly unusual. Nevertheless, despite their "recent vintage," each had undergone a considerable degree of democratization. These examples, then, are disturbing. For whatever their flaws, Weimar Germany, the pre-Mussolini Italian constitutional monarchy, and republican Spain were definitely democratizing states, if not full-fledged democracies from today's perspective. The question that arises, then, is: If these democratizing states of interwar Europe could succumb to revolution, is there any reason to think that the democratizing states of the post–Cold War era are invulnerable to it?

If any of today's newly democratizing (or redemocratizing) states were overthrown by revolution, those wedded to the assumption that democracy and revolution are inversely related are likely to advance either of two explanations: (1) the government in power was not really democratic, and hence was vulnerable to revolution; or (2) the government in power really was democratic, but it was overthrown by a coup d'état, conspiracy, or some other machination short of a "genuine" revolution. The theory that democracy and revolution are inversely related may thus be (or seem) protected, but newly democratizing states are clearly not. Even assuming that the theory is correct, it is uncertain what the threshold of democratization is that, once crossed, reduces or eliminates a state's vulnerability to revolution. And if this threshold cannot be identified (or perhaps even if it can), then judging which present-day democratizing states have crossed it is obviously problematic.

Because "newly democratizing" covers a gray area between authoritarian and fully democratic, it may be too much to expect the assumption about democracy and revolution being inversely related to be fully operative. Nor does it seem surprising that newly democratizing states are more vulnerable to being overthrown by something (whether or not it is revolution) than long-established democracies. But if democracy and revolution are not necessarily inversely related, is it possible that even a long-established one could succumb to revolution?

This has never happened. Of course, this does not mean that it could not happen in the future. But just as with the possibility of war between two established democracies, it seems highly unlikely. Nevertheless, it appears that revolution against a long-established democracy is at least conceivable under extreme circumstances.

Conceivable, but how likely? One way to address this question is to examine how, by relaxing the assumption that democracy and revolution are inversely related, the likelihood of revolution if democratization advances in a linear fashion or if it expands and contracts cyclically might be affected.

Let us begin first with the theory that democracy can expand and contract in cycles, though fewer democracies can be expected to revert to authoritarianism than make the transition from authoritarianism to democracy. Assuming that democracy and revolution may not be inversely related, revolution against partially or incompletely democratic states, as Selbin argues, appears possible. It is even conceivable that a long-established democracy could succumb to revolution under a combination of extreme circumstances such as economic collapse, humiliating military defeat, and external support for the revolutionaries who seek to overthrow a democratic government—one or more of which circumstances was present when fascist revolutions overthrew democratizing governments in Italy, Germany, and then Spain (Carsten 1971; Eatwell 1995).

But even if this possibility is admitted, it is difficult to imagine, after the twentieth century's horrible experience with nondemocratic revolutionary regimes, that people in general will ever prefer authoritarianism to democracy for long, if at all. While relaxing the assumption that revolution and democracy are inversely related allows for the possibility of revolution against democratic governments, the main targets of revolution in a world where democracy expands and contracts cyclically are still likely to be authoritarian governments. Thus, relaxing the assumption that democracy and revolution are inversely related generally supports Selbin's prediction that the age of revolution is not over in a world where democracy expands and contracts cyclically. On the other hand, neither does it appear that relaxing this assumption would necessarily lead to more revolution in such a world.

This may not be the case, however, if we assume that democracy advances in a linear fashion. In a world where all or nearly all countries are democratic, democracy's superiority to dictatorship may appear obvious, but no longer relevant. What may be relevant in such a world instead is whether any given state is "more" or "less" democratic than others. Virtually any form of democracy may appear superior to any form of dictatorship now. But in a world where democracies are only compared with one another, differences that now seem small may well loom large. While accepted now, systems of government with a powerful executive and weak legislature, or with electoral systems that result in the over-representation of less populous provinces and the under-representation of more populous ones, may come to be regarded as utterly intolerable in a largely democratic world.

Just as the notion of what constitutes a democracy has evolved over the past two centuries, it may further evolve in the future. And just as certain features of yesterday's democracies—such as limiting the voting franchise to males—were once commonly accepted but are now considered intolerable, certain common features of today's democracies may be considered intolerable in the future.

If we assume that democracy and revolution are inversely related, then the only way for democracies to shed old practices and adopt new ones is through the operation of the existing constitutional arrangements. However, in some democracies (especially the United States), bringing about major—or even minor—political change is extremely difficult. A minority that benefits from preserving the status quo can—and often has—been able to block change desired by the majority. For example, the filibuster is one method by which the minority (albeit a sizeable one) can block action by the majority in the U.S. Senate—a practice that is clearly undemocratic but which the Senate has shown no sign of abandoning.

It is conceivable that in a largely democratic world, the reform of existing democracies may become a popular cause, but the existing democratic institutions may be unable to enact them due to the unwillingness of the over-represented provinces or minorities that they empower to surrender their privileged position. In the United States, for example, each state elects two U.S. senators no matter how great or how small its population. Voters in more populous states might feel that a fairer distribution would allocate senators to each state on the basis of its percentage of the total U.S. population, as occurs in the allocation of congressmen to the House of Representatives. California might then have ten or more Senate seats while the least populous states might only be entitled to one each, or may even have to share one with a neighboring state. It is highly unlikely, however, that the less populous states would ever agree to give up a Senate seat so that more populous ones could be more fairly represented.[1]

As their evolution has shown, democracies are capable of major reform, though this usually occurs only slowly and gradually. On the other hand, certain imperfections or limitations on democracy have largely been tolerated; they have not been so severe that they have led to widespread protest against their persistence, or even the demand for their reform. In a mainly democratic world, however, it may be that publics will be unwilling to tolerate either existing limitations on democracy or existing democratic institutions that prove unwilling or unable to remove them expeditiously. It is possible, then, that a democratic revolution may occur in order to rapidly reform an existing democracy whose institutions are incapable of reforming themselves to the satisfaction of the majority.

A democratic revolution to reform an existing democracy need not be—indeed, should not be—a violent one. It might be more akin to the largely peaceful revolutions that swept through most of Eastern Europe in 1989. It might come about through, as in Eastern Europe, a mass peaceful general strike that forces the institutions of the old order, despite their own preference for preserving the status quo, to enact popular demands for reform even if this results in these institutions being substantially modified or even replaced.

In a largely democratic world, it is more likely that democratic revolution would occur against newly democratizing states—where the balance of power among the institutions of government has either been poorly articulated constitutionally or skewed in favor of what has been termed a "superpresidency"—than in long-established democracies where checks and balances among government institutions have largely been worked out and are clearly understood. Nevertheless, the resistance to rapid change on the part of long-established democratic governments may result in their also being vulnerable to democratic revolution—especially if it is understood that this sort of revolution is absolutely and unquestionably democratic.

Assuming that progress toward democratization occurs in a linear fashion and that democracy and revolution are not inversely related, then, supports Selbin's contention that the age of revolution is not over. The only type of revolution likely to occur if both these conditions were true, however, would be democratic revolution aimed at improving and reforming existing democratic governments—a very different type of revolution than the more traditional peasant revolution that Selbin appears to envisage.

Ultimately, answering the question about whether the age of revolution is over depends upon what is meant by the term "revolution." If it is understood to be characterized by large-scale peasant uprisings, then it is doubtful that revolution can long persist into the future: peasants are moving to the cities and, whether quickly or slowly, becoming educated and embourgeoised. Irrespective of whether they live in democracies or autocracies, the time may soon be arriving (if it hasn't already) that the peasant proportion of the population in most countries will not be large enough to undertake uprisings capable of overthrowing governments.

Seeing revolution solely as peasant uprising, however, is an unnecessarily static conception. A more dynamic conception of revolution would recognize that the nature of revolution changes with changing conditions. As peasants have moved to the cities, they have often found it extremely difficult to find meaningful employment or acceptance. According to Olivier Roy, it is just such people who in the past two decades have supported undemocratic Islamic revolution—largely an urban phenomenon in almost all the countries where it has occurred or been attempted (1994, 50). Finally, the peaceful revolutions of 1989 in Eastern Europe were primarily the work of highly urbanized, democratically oriented populaces (Markoff 1996, 95–6).

In this sense, revolution resembles democracy in that it is something that is not static, but is capable of dynamic change and redefinition. And because both democracy and revolution are evolving phenomena, it is impossible to state definitively whether or not the assumption that democracy and revolution are inversely related is permanently valid. Since these two phenomena are subject to change, the relationship between them would also appear to be so.

Yet while the changing nature of democracy over time is something that is widely recognized, a relatively static conception of revolution continues to hold sway, even among scholars specializing on this subject. For those who cling to the static conception of violent peasant uprising as the only true form of revolution, then the disappearance of the peasantry alone must necessarily result in the age of revolution soon being over. But for those willing to embrace a more dynamic conception of revolution that includes the largely peaceful uprisings of 1989 in Eastern Europe, then the age of revolution can neither be said to be over as Goodwin argues nor to "remain the same as it ever was" as Selbin maintains, but to have entered a new phase.

CHAPTER 6

RESPONDING TO REVOLUTION IN THE POST–COLD WAR ERA

Reflections on Jeane Kirkpatrick

PART AND PARCEL OF ANY UNDERSTANDING of revolution is an understanding of how status quo powers react to it. In general, it is safe to say, status quo powers have felt threatened by the occurrence of revolution. But they have felt even more threatened when a revolution, after coming to power in one country, spreads to others and appears likely to spread to yet others still. The more revolution spreads, the more the influence of status quo powers is likely to recede. The ultimate fear of status quo governments is that if revolution spreads far enough, it can threaten their status as great powers, or even their very existence.[1]

Clearly, status quo powers are not going to remain idle if they think (and they always do) that the spread of revolution actually or even potentially threatens their interests, as they define them. They will attempt, at minimum, to halt or contain the spread of revolution before it can further damage these interests. The ability of status quo powers to do this successfully depends, in part, on the resources they have available for this task. But even the possession of abundant resources by no means guarantees that a status quo power can contain the spread of revolution. The government of a status quo power must also have the ability to use such resources effectively, which in turn presupposes an accurate understanding of how to contain revolution.

Since this study is about revolution in the post–Cold War era, it will focus on the most important status quo power at present: the United States. Containing the spread of revolution—primarily of the Marxist-Leninist variety—was one of the principle aims of American foreign policy during the Cold War. With the end of the Cold War, most Marxist-Leninist regimes collapsed. The few remaining ones are either uninterested in or unable to spread revolution. Nevertheless, in the post–Cold War era, the United States government (along with other status quo powers) remains deeply concerned about containing the spread of revolution—primarily of the Islamic fundamentalist variety.

Leaving aside the question of whether it is desirable for the United States or any other status quo government to contain the spread of revolution (highly desirable from the viewpoint of the status quo powers and highly undesirable from the viewpoint of revolutionaries), the question to be examined is: does the U.S. government know how to contain post–Cold War revolution effectively?

The question is pertinent because, while the collapse of communism in 1989–91 brought about the end of the Cold War, the United States did not succeed in containing the spread of Marxist revolution in the Third World before it ended, especially during the decade of the 1970s. And since the United States seeks to prevent the spread of Islamic revolution in the 1990s in basically the same way that it sought to prevent the spread of Marxist revolution after the 1973 American withdrawal from Indochina, the logic of the post–Vietnam American effort to contain revolution needs to be examined with regard to its applicability in the post–Cold War era.

THE KIRKPATRICK LOGIC

Jeane Kirkpatrick's "Dictatorships and Double Standards" (1979) was hardly the first articulation of American containment policy.

Indeed, it came rather late in the Cold War—only ten years before its end. (That it would end through the collapse of communism, of course, was not expected then.) Kirkpatrick's article, however, differed from earlier statements of containment in two important respects.

First, earlier statements of containment, including the famous "X" article by George Kennan (1947), focused primarily on the nature of the Soviet Union and on preventing it from invading other countries on the periphery of its sphere of influence, especially in Europe. These statements often paid relatively little attention to the Third World. Kirkpatrick, by contrast, focused on the conditions in the Third World in which the Soviet-American competition played out.

Second, the earlier statements about containment assumed, either explicitly or implicitly, that the United States could intervene militarily to halt the spread of revolution. Kirkpatrick, by contrast, was aware of the difficulty that American domestic politics posed for launching large-scale U.S. military intervention to quell revolution in the post–Vietnam era. Twenty years after the appearance of her article, this condition still holds (notwithstanding the 1991 Desert Storm operation—launched to reverse an invasion, not quell a revolution).

What, then, was the Kirkpatrick logic? Her article was written in response to what she saw as the Carter Administration's policy of undercutting pro-American right-wing Third World regimes because they were not democratic, and doing nothing to prevent them from being replaced by rabidly anti-American and undemocratic regimes, as occurred in both Nicaragua and Iran in 1979.

She argued that while democracy was obviously preferable to right-wing authoritarianism, right-wing authoritarianism was preferable to left-wing totalitarianism. Authoritarian regimes, she pointed out, allowed some degree of freedom, especially in the economic sphere, while totalitarian ones allowed no freedom in any sphere. Limited as it was, then, the degree of freedom existing in authoritarian regimes meant that they possessed much greater potential for democratic transformation than did totalitarian regimes. This potential for democratic transformation in authoritarian regimes, however, could not be realized when they were fighting for survival against totalitarian revolutionaries (especially ones that were externally armed). Just as democratization in the West was a long drawn-out process, she argued, it could not be expected to develop quickly in the Third World either (1979, 44).

The United States, then, must help somewhat free authoritarian regimes defeat totalitarian revolutionaries in order for democratization to have the opportunity to emerge later under more favorable circumstances. Cutting back or ending support to authoritarian regimes fighting externally backed totalitarian revolutionaries would result in the downfall of the former and the rise of the latter, who would block progress toward democratization far more effectively than the authoritarian regime they overthrew.

Although published in 1979, Kirkpatrick's article was an accurate description of how the United States sought to contain the spread of Marxist revolution most of the time in most of the Third World. For even in the earlier part of the Cold War, when it was more possible, Washington preferred not to undertake this task through direct U.S. military intervention. This was simply less cost effective than making sure that our authoritarian allies were strong enough militarily to defeat any totalitarian revolutionary movement and strong enough economically to undercut the latter's potential appeal. If the United States could do this successfully, then the need for direct U.S. military intervention might not even arise—thus avoiding the difficult domestic problems in the United States that resulted from American intervention in Vietnam.

IN RETROSPECT

Twenty years later, it is obvious that several elements of the Kirkpatrick logic were incorrect. First and foremost, although she had argued that they could not do so, many anti-American totalitarian regimes were transformed into democratic—or at least democratizing—states following the 1989–91 collapse of communism. Formerly Marxist-ruled countries that have made the most progress toward democracy include Poland, the Czech Republic,

Hungary, Romania, Slovenia, Estonia, Latvia, Lithuania, and Nicaragua. Although their transitions have been more problematic, significant democratization has also occurred in Russia and Ukraine as well as in other former Soviet republics. Even China and Vietnam, where totalitarian regimes remain firmly and stubbornly in place, have allowed substantial economic change through the rise of domestic capitalism and economic interaction with the rest of the world. These two countries now more closely resemble what Kirkpatrick described as authoritarian regimes. In 1979, she did not anticipate that totalitarian regimes were capable of even this more modest form of transformation.

Second, while Kirkpatrick proclaimed that democratization was an extremely long, slow process, the experience of the last two decades demonstrates that it can occur extremely quickly. This was shown not only in several formerly totalitarian Marxist cases, but also in some pro-American authoritarian ones such as Spain and Portugal in the 1970s, and the Philippines, South Korea, and Chile in the 1980s.

Third, while many totalitarian regimes that Kirkpatrick did not expect to do so have undergone significant democratization, many authoritarian regimes that she described in 1979 as being more likely to democratize have not. Little or no progress toward democratization during the last two decades has been made in such pro-American authoritarian regimes as Indonesia, Egypt, Saudi Arabia, Oman, and the United Arab Emirates. While relatively (though not completely) free parliamentary elections are held in Morocco, Jordan, and Kuwait, their elected parliaments have very little ability to constrain the actions of their nonelected executives. Further, because the countries mentioned here are either rich in oil or strategically located (or both), Washington has firmly supported their authoritarian regimes, and this American support appears to have contributed to their success in resisting the popular demand for democratization that has toppled so many totalitarian and authoritarian ones in countries less important to the United States.

Fourth, since it is obvious in retrospect that totalitarian regimes could undergo rapid democratization while authoritarian ones could avoid it, the distinction Kirkpatrick made between them is not a meaningful one. Indeed, instead of describing some fundamental difference between regime types, the term "authoritarian" in Kirkpatrick's lexicon is primarily a synonym for pro-American, while "totalitarian" is primarily a synonym for anti-American. In retrospect, it is evident that Kirkpatrick's authoritarian regimes that have most successfully resisted democratization are in fact more totalitarian than her totalitarian regimes which did not.

IMPLICATIONS

Kirkpatrick should not be especially criticized just because her containment theory did not anticipate events 20, or even 10, years in advance. The collapse of communism was almost universally unanticipated. Even those few who said it would eventually collapse did not indicate that it would occur when it did. As discussed earlier, later events would show that Kirkpatrick's assumptions about the nature of Third World regimes and the prospects for their democratization were simply incorrect.

Pointing this out, however, is not merely an academic exercise. For despite its incorrect assumptions, the United States continues to apply the Kirkpatrick logic in its effort to contain the spread of post–Cold War revolution, especially in the Muslim world. Washington fears the coming to power of totalitarian (anti-American) Islamic fundamentalist revolutionaries in this region, where so many countries happen to possess abundant reserves of petroleum. So it is here in particular that the United States supports authoritarian (pro-American) regimes such as those in Saudi Arabia, Egypt, Morocco, and Indonesia.

An obvious question arises: Is there any problem in pursuing the Kirkpatrick logic to contain the spread of revolution when several premises of this logic are flawed? For whatever its inconsistencies, pursuing the Kirkpatrick logic clearly did not prevent the collapse of communism a decade ago. It is even possible to argue that by pursuing the Kirkpatrick logic, the United States prevented the further spread of Marxist revolution, and thereby denied Moscow important resources with which it might have further damaged American interests and possibly even prevented the collapse of communism.

Such a contention, of course, is highly debatable. Certainly, though, the Kirkpatrick logic's insistence on containing the spread of revolution linked to a totalitarian state appears highly prudent. The fact that communism collapsed and communist regimes underwent democratization was an unexpected bonus that did not obviate the need to contain the Marxist revolutionary wave while it was strong and making aggressive efforts to expand.

This would suggest that despite whatever possibility exists of Iran democratizing in the future (or even that it has begun this process already), the most prudent course of action for the United States is to continue resisting the expansion of the Islamic fundamentalist revolutionary wave. For in addition to being highly undemocratic and virulently anti-American, the Islamic fundamentalist revolutionary movements operating in other countries are less subject to Iranian influence than Third World Marxist revolutionary movements were to Soviet influence (Katz 1997, 75–81). In other words, while the collapse of communism in the USSR also led to the collapse of almost all remaining Marxist-Leninist revolutionary movements, significant progress toward democratization in Iran (which, as the communist experience demonstrated and the election of a moderate to the Iranian presidency indicates, is certainly possible) might have little impact on totalitarian Islamic revolutionary movements seeking to overthrow pro-American authoritarian regimes in predominantly Sunni Muslim countries.

This would further suggest, then, that the United States must continue to resist the expansion of totalitarian anti-American Islamic fundamentalist revolution through, as Kirkpatrick advised, strong U.S. support to the authoritarian pro-American regimes of the Muslim world. Indeed, the United States would appear to have little choice but to support these authoritarian regimes since in the Muslim world there are very few democracies, and most of these few are what Fareed Zakaria termed "illiberal democracies" that closely resemble authoritarian regimes (1997). And finally, the fact that so many of these pro-American authoritarian regimes in the Muslim world are oil rich themselves or abut countries that are means that internal threats to them have far greater consequences for America and the West than did Marxist revolutions in countries possessing far less economic or strategic importance to the West, such as Cuba, Nicaragua, Mozambique, Ethiopia, Afghanistan, or Cambodia. Now more than ever, there appears to be a compelling case for applying the Kirkpatrick logic, at least in the Muslim world.

It is here, however, that the flaws in the Kirkpatrick logic can have serious negative consequences for the United States. Although a sharp decline in American support for an authoritarian regime may soon lead to its downfall, it does not necessarily follow, as she argued, that strong U.S. support for an authoritarian regime will lead to its survival. One of the cases she focused on in "Dictatorships and Double Standards" illustrates this. Despite its emphasis on human rights, the Carter Administration strongly supported the Shah of Iran. Although it is often pointed out that President Carter advised the Shah not to use force against his opponents, the Shah himself appeared unwilling to do so throughout the crisis that led to his downfall. According to Gary Sick's detailed account of U.S.-Iranian relations during these years, the Shah appeared to be as concerned about the possibility of being overthrown by his own officers as by the revolutionaries (1986, 198–201).

What this demonstrates is that even massive arms transfers to an authoritarian regime (such as the United States transferred to the Shah) will not serve to protect it if the ruler will not allow his officers to make use of them for fear that they will further their own aims at his expense. Nor will such arms transfers prove useful if the armed forces become infused with the desire for political change, and either refuse to fire upon the regime's opponents or even use Western-supplied weapons to overthrow the regime they are supposed to protect. It was primarily Western—not Soviet— weapons that were used in the coups d'état that overthrew pro-Western governments and brought anti-Western revolutionary regimes to power in Egypt (1952), Syria (1956), Iraq (1958), Libya (1969), and Sudan (1969).

The problem with the Kirkpatrick logic, then, is that the American support it insists be provided to underwrite pro-American authoritarian regimes may not serve this purpose, or worse, may even be used to undermine such regimes by their own armed forces. This might not occur in all cases where the United States is supporting pro-American authoritarian regimes. But past experience suggests that it would be foolish to expect that all American-backed authoritarian regimes will be invulnerable to revolutionary opponents—especially those within their own armed forces.

The research of Timothy Lomperis (1996, 317–18) and Jeff Goodwin (1998) suggests that democratically elected governments are the least vulnerable to revolution. But Kirkpatrick was undoubtedly right when she wrote that democratization was unlikely to succeed "at a time when the incumbent government is fighting for its life against violent adversaries" (1979, 44). The most sensible policy for the United States, then, would be to encourage pro-American authoritarian regimes to democratize before an anti-American revolutionary opposition can become strong enough to thwart such an effort—especially since, contrary to Kirkpatrick's expectations, several transitions to democracy by totalitarian regimes as well as authoritarian ones have demonstrated that this can take place quickly.

In the past, however, the United States has not made any serious effort to promote democratization in oil-rich Muslim states, but has firmly supported pro-American authoritarian regimes there instead. Nor does this appear likely to change. The reason for this is understandable: since America and the West are so dependent economically on these oil-rich authoritarian regimes, the consequences of democratization efforts gone wrong are much greater in these states than in those with less economic significance. Thus, supporting the existing pro-American authoritarian regimes in the oil-rich states of the Muslim world is seen in Washington as much less risky than promoting democratization in them.

Yet while designed to avoid risk, it must be recognized that there is serious risk involved over the long term of supporting oil-rich pro-American authoritarian states that suppress all of their domestic opponents. Especially now when progress toward democracy—and American support for it—are visible in so many other parts of the world, the lack of such progress in the oil-rich Muslim world stands out as an anomaly. The long-term risk Washington runs is that through not pressing authoritarian regimes to democratize when they are not facing significant opposition from "totalitarian" Islamic fundamentalist revolutionaries may result in forgoing the opportunity to promote their democratization if and when they do.

For if Islamic fundamentalist forces grow so strong that the authoritarian regimes they seek to overthrow cannot defeat them even with substantial arms transfers from America and the West, the United States will then be left with the stark choice between (1) undertaking direct—possibly long-term—military intervention to defeat the revolutionaries (which may or may not succeed), or (2) not doing so and thus allowing the revolutionaries to win. And given the American public's well known aversion to open-ended military intervention to protect authoritarian regimes against their internal opponents, Washington may again be forced to make the latter choice, just as the Carter Administration was in the late 1970s.

NOTES

CHAPTER 1

1. Even from his perspective so long ago, Aristotle noted that the division of society into classes was something ancient (275–6). He also noted the existence of a middle class, government by which he saw as least likely to degenerate into tyranny (172–3). He observed, however, that the middle class was "frequently small" (174). This description of the relative unimportance of the middle class did not become invalid until the eighteenth through twentieth centuries in the West and until very recently elsewhere. And, of course, there are still countries where this description of its role remains valid.

2. Moore considered the nineteenth-century American Civil War, not the eighteenth-century war for independence, to be the real American Revolution. Similarly, Moore did not consider India's largely peaceful struggle for independence to be a revolution; the Indian Revolution was something that was yet to come.

3. Moore wrote:

> Germany and, even more, Japan were trying to solve a problem that was inherently insoluble, to modernize without changing their social structures. The only way out of this dilemma was militarism, which united the upper classes. Militarism intensified a climate of international conflict, which in turn made industrial advance all the more imperative ... Ultimately these systems crashed in an attempt at foreign expansion, but not until they had tried to make reaction popular in the form of fascism (1966, 441–2).

4. If Moore had made this prediction about Iran instead of India, the 1979 victory of the Islamic fundamentalist revolution there, whose

leaders rejected both East and West, would have made him appear extraordinarily prescient.

5. This book had a powerful impact on those of us who were students during the Vietnam war and its immediate aftermath. Skocpol's acknowledgement of how reading the book as an undergraduate at Michigan State University inspired her reminds me of my own reaction to the book when I first read it as an undergraduate in a class on comparative revolutions in the spring of 1975. Moore's book was presented by the professor as the Truth, and was indeed received by us students as being something akin to a revelation. This reverential attitude toward *Social Origins* was also in evidence in the MIT Political Science Department among the graduate students and at least one professor who lectured on Moore in the late 1970s.

6. A long review of *Social Origins* by Skocpol, originally published in 1973, critiqued the book itself and other critiques of it (1994, 25–54).

7. Just two years before the collapse of communism, Paul Kennedy warned of the impending decline of American power. He wrote, "By far the most worrying situation of all . . . lies just to the south of the United States, and makes the Polish 'crisis' for the USSR seem small by comparison. There is simply no equivalent in the world for the present state of Mexican-United States relations" (1987, 517).

8. While the Soviet Union often provided lavish military assistance to Marxist-Leninist regimes in the Third World, it provided much less assistance (in many cases, none) to Marxist-Leninist revolutionary movements there (Golan 1988, 261–91; MacFarlane 1990). Forrest Colburn has shown that many Third World Marxist leaders did not acquire their Marxism in the Soviet Union or other communist countries, but in Western Europe and the United States (1994, 20–35).

9. There is a debate, however, over whether the United States or Western Europe was more responsible for these democratic transformations (Huntington 1991, 98; Schmitter 1995).

10. Sudan's Arab nationalist regime was overthrown in 1985 and was eventually replaced by an Islamic fundamentalist government in 1989.

11. The Soviet "united front" strategy, though, usually failed since, as Franz Borkenau noted, it was based on a "childlike conviction that your adversary will not understand your intentions, though you express them quite openly, that he will continue to cooperate with you as long as *you* want it, and allow himself to be overthrown when it suits *you*" (cited in Rodman 1994, 35).

12. With regard to the cases of "people's war" insurgency that he studied, Lomperis argued that "wherever the insurgents were able to make successful belief-level appeals to national legitimacy, they won, as in at least one Vietnam case and China; and wherever such appeals eluded them, as in Greece, the Philippines, and Malaya, they lost" (1996, 274–5).

CHAPTER 2

1. Leszek Kolakowski (1978) authored a massive study examining the breadth of nineteenth- and twentieth-century Marxist thought.

2. See, for example, Aslund (1995) on Ukraine; Geller and Connor (1996) on Uzbekistan; Jones (1996) on Georgia; Haghayeghi (1997) on Kyrgyzstan; Dudwick (1997, 99–101) on Armenia; Altstadt (1997, 137–41) on Azerbaijan; Olcott (1997, 216–18) on Kazakhstan; and Ochs (1997, 340–6) on Turkmenistan. Three successive visits to Almaty during the early 1990s demonstrated to me just how rapidly and enthusiastically the ex-communist leadership of Kazakhstan was embracing capitalism.

CHAPTER 3

1. In the three-island Federal Islamic Republic of the Comoros, a movement has arisen on the two smaller islands "to demand what amounts to recolonization by France," which still rules the nearby island of Mayotte (Trueheart 1997). It does not appear likely, however, that this movement will succeed or, more importantly, that it will inspire similar demands for recolonization elsewhere.

CHAPTER 4

1. Theda Skocpol, for example, asked, "What society . . . lacks widespread relative deprivation of one sort or another? . . . Ironically, theoretical approaches that set out to avoid the pitfalls of a too-historical approach to revolutions can end up providing little more than pointers toward various factors that case analysts might want to take into account, with no valid way to favor certain explanations over others" (1979, 34). See also Sederberg (1994, 122–7).

Stephen Brush (1996) examined the changing evaluation of Gurr's theory after its publication. He pointed out that while at first widely accepted, Gurr's relative deprivation theory came under criticism from sociologists and political scientists for not being supported by empirical evidence. Brush found, though, that many of those who rejected the theory cited nonempirical reasons instead of empirical ones. The theory, however, remains generally accepted by psychologists. Perhaps the most unusual aspect in the saga of this theory is that Gurr himself later developed an ambivalent attitude toward it.

Part of the problem is that the theory, as Gurr first stated it, was too ambitious in what it attempted to explain. Clearly, as I argue here, other factors need to be present for a sense of relative deprivation to lead to a successful revolution. In my view, though, the concept of relative deprivation insofar as it describes a psychological state is extremely useful for understanding the motives of those who undertake different kinds of revolution, including nationalist secessionist revolution.

2. On how this situation arose historically, see Katz (1993).

3. Long before the Cold War, though, the United States did support—indeed, engineered—the 1903 secession of Panama from Colombia. Considering that the United States acquired direct control over what would become the Panama Canal Zone as well as a highly intrusive role in Panamanian politics, this episode cannot be considered an example of American support for secessionist nationalism, but as an example of American overseas colonial expansion (T. Smith 1994, 65–8).

4. The Turkish Cypriot Republic's secession from the rest of Cyprus in 1974 might be considered a fourth case of successful secession during the Cold War. The establishment of this state, however, occurred primarily as a result of an invasion from Turkey. And unlike the Indian troops that withdrew from Bangladesh shortly after helping establish its independence, Turkish forces have remained in this part of Cyprus ever since 1974. The "independence" of the Turkish Cypriot Republic, then, is less an example of successful secession than of successful invasion (Lenczowski 1980, 164).

5. "Generally," though, does not mean always. In 1996, the United States reportedly began providing assistance via Ethiopia, Eritrea, and Uganda to secessionist rebels fighting against the Islamic fundamentalist regime in Sudan (Ottaway 1996).

6. The leader of Ghana's independence movement, Kwame Nkrumah, described his own "Positive Action" campaign as being "based on the principle of absolute non-violence, as used by Gandhi in India" (Nkrumah [1957] 1971, 112).

7. The Soviet Union had several types of administrative subdivisions. The most important were the "union republics," which enjoyed the theoretical right to secede from the USSR. It was the 15 union republics that became independent states in 1991. But there were also "autonomous republics," "autonomous regions," and "national districts" for smaller ethnic groups, which did not have even the theoretical right to secede (G. Smith 1992, 131).

8. As Hurst Hannum put it, "the shattering of the Soviet Union, Yugoslavia, Czechoslovakia, and Ethiopia within the past decade is a precedent not lost on many 'nations' that would be states" (1998, 13).

CHAPTER 5

1. Article V of the U.S. Constitution, which sets forth the process by which the Constitution may be amended, specifically enjoins "that no State, without its consent, shall be deprived of its equal suffrage in the Senate."

CHAPTER 6

1. On relations between status quo and revolutionary powers, see Conge (1996); Walt (1996); and Katz (1997, 117–35).

BIBLIOGRAPHY

Abrahamian, Ervand. 1993. *Khomeinism: Essays on the Islamic Republic.* Berkeley: University of California Press.

Altstadt, Audrey L. 1997. "Azerbaijan's Struggle toward Democracy." In *Conflict, Cleavage, and Change in Central Asia and the Caucasus,* edited by Karen Dawisha and Bruce Parrott, pp. 110–155. Cambridge: Cambridge University Press.

Andaya, Barbara Watson, and Leonard Y. Andaya. 1982. *A History of Malaysia.* London: Macmillan Press.

Aristotle. 1962. *The Politics.* Trans. T. A. Sinclair. Harmondsworth: Penguin Books.

Arthur, Paul. 1996. "Anglo-Irish Relations." In *Northern Ireland Politics,* edited by Arthur Aughey and Duncan Morrow, pp. 113–120. London: Longman.

Aslund, Anders. 1995. "Eurasia Letter: Ukraine's Turnaround." *Foreign Policy,* no. 100 (Fall):125–143.

Ayubi, Nazih. 1991. *Political Islam: Religion and Politics in the Arab World.* London: Routledge.

Bakhash, Shaul. 1990. *The Reign of the Ayatollahs: Iran and the Islamic Revolution,* rev. ed. New York: Basic Books.

Barkey, Henri J., and Graham E. Fuller. 1997. "Turkey's Kurdish Question: Critical Turning Points and Missed Opportunities." *Middle East Journal* 51:59–79.

Beddoes, Zanny Minton. 1998. "A Caspian Gamble." *The Economist,* February 7, S1-S18.

Bernstein, Richard, and Ross H. Munro. 1997. "The Coming Conflict with America." *Foreign Affairs* 76 (March/April):18–32.

Binder, Leonard. 1988. *Islamic Liberalism: A Critique of Development Ideologies.* Chicago: University of Chicago Press.

Blank, Stephen. 1996. "Russian Democracy and the West after Chechnya." *Comparative Strategy* 15:11–29.

Brinton, Crane. 1965. *The Anatomy of Revolution*, 3rd ed. New York: Vintage Books.

Brown, W. Norman. 1972. *The United States and India, Pakistan, Bangladesh*, 3rd ed. Cambridge, MA: Harvard University Press.

Brush, Stephen G. 1996. "Dynamics of Theory Change in the Social Sciences: Relative Deprivation and Collective Violence." *Journal of Conflict Resolution* 40:525–545.

Brzezinski, Zbigniew. 1983. *Power and Principle: Memoirs of the National Security Adviser, 1977–1981*. New York: Farrar, Straus and Giroux.

———. 1989. *The Grand Failure: The Birth and Death of Communism in the Twentieth Century*. New York: Charles Scribner's Sons.

Brzezinski, Zbigniew, *et al.* 1997. "Differentiated Containment." *Foreign Affairs* 76 (May/June):20–30.

Cardoso, Fernando Jorge. 1994. "Portugal-Africa Bilateral Relations in a Changing Environment." In *Africa and Europe: Relations of Two Continents in Transition*, edited by Stefan Brune *et al.*, pp. 109–119. Munster/Hamburg: Lit Verlag.

Carley, Patricia. 1997. "U.S. Responses to Self-Determination Movements: Strategies for Nonviolent Outcomes and Alternatives to Secession." Peaceworks No. 16. Washington, D.C.: United States Institute of Peace.

Carsten, F. L. 1971. *The Rise of Fascism*. Berkeley: University of California Press.

Castañeda, Jorge G. 1996. "Mexico's Circle of Misery." *Foreign Affairs* 75 (July/August):92–105.

Chan, Anita, and Robert A. Senser. 1997. "China's Troubled Workers." *Foreign Affairs* 76 (March/April):104–117.

Colburn, Forrest D. 1994. *The Vogue of Revolution in Poor Countries*. Princeton: Princeton University Press.

Conge, Patrick J. 1996. *From Revolution to War: State Relations in a World of Change*. Ann Arbor: University of Michigan Press.

Cooper, Kenneth J. 1998. "Hindu Party's Agenda Raises Troubling Issues for Many Indians." *Washington Post*, May 18, p. A13.

Crowther, William. 1994. "Moldova After Independence." *Current History* 93:342–347.

Dawisha, Adeed. 1986. *The Arab Radicals*. New York: Council on Foreign Relations.

Dawisha, Karen, and Bruce Parrott. 1994. *Russia and the New States of Eurasia: The Politics of Upheaval*. Cambridge: Cambridge University Press.

Dobson, Richard B. 1996. "Is Russia Turning the Corner? Changing Russian Public Opinion, 1991–1996." U.S. Information Agency, Office of Research and Media Reaction, Russia, Ukraine, and Commonwealth Branch. R-7–96.

Doran, Charles F. 1996. "Will Canada Unravel?" *Foreign Affairs* 75 (September/October):97–109.

Dresser, Denise. 1997. "Mexico: Uneasy, Uncertain, Unpredictable." *Current History* 96:49–54.

————. 1998. "Mexico After the July 6 Election: Neither Heaven nor Hell." *Current History* 97:55–60.

Dudwick, Nora. 1997. "Political Transformations in Postcommunist Armenia: Images and Realities." In *Conflict, Cleavage, and Change in Central Asia and the Caucasus,* edited by Karen Dawisha and Bruce Parrott, pp. 69–109. Cambridge: Cambridge University Press.

Eatwell, Roger. 1995. *Fascism: A History.* New York: Penguin Books.

Elliott, David W. P. 1995. "Vietnam Faces the Future." *Current History* 94:412–419.

Fandy, Mamoun. 1994. "Egypt's Islamic Group: Regional Revenge?" *Middle East Journal* 48:607–625.

Farhi, Farideh. 1990. *States and Urban-Based Revolutions: Iran and Nicaragua.* Urbana: University of Illinois Press.

Figes, Orlando. 1996. *A People's Tragedy: The Russian Revolution, 1891–1924.* New York: Penguin Books.

Foran, John. 1994. "The Iranian Revolution of 1977–79: A Challenge for Social Theory." In *A Century of Revolution: Social Movements in Iran,* edited by John Foran, pp. 160–188. Minneapolis: University of Minnesota Press.

Fukuyama, Francis. 1992. *The End of History and the Last Man.* New York: Free Press.

Garthoff, Raymond. 1994. *The Great Transition: American-Soviet Relations and the End of the Cold War.* Washington, D.C.: Brookings Institution.

Gebicki, Wojciech, and Anna Maria Gebicki. 1995. "Central Europe: A Shift to the Left?" *Survival* 37 (Autumn):126–138.

Geller, Tatyana S., and John T. Connor, Jr. 1996. "Uzbekistan Lays the Foundation for a Securities Market." *Central Asia Monitor,* no. 5:27–33.

Gerber, Haim. 1987. *The Social Origins of the Modern Middle East.* Boulder, CO: Lynne Rienner.

Gladney, Dru C. 1997. "Rumblings from the Uyghur." *Current History* 96:287–290.

Golan, Galia. 1988. *The Soviet Union and National Liberation Movements in the Third World.* Boston: Unwin Hyman.

Goldstone, Jack A. 1980. "Theories of Revolution: The Third Generation." *World Politics* 32:425–453.

———. 1991. *Revolution and Rebellion in the Early Modern World.* Berkeley: University of California Press.

———. 1997. "Population Growth and Revolutionary Crises." In *Theorizing Revolutions,* edited by John Foran, pp. 102–120. London: Routledge.

Goodwin, Jeff. 1998. "Is the Age of Revolutions Over?" Paper presented at the International Studies Association Annual Convention, Minneapolis, March 21.

Grant, Robert P. 1996. "France's New Relationship with NATO." *Survival* 38 (Spring):58–80.

Greenfeld, Liah. 1992. *Nationalism: Five Roads to Modernity.* Cambridge, MA: Harvard University Press.

Gurr, Ted Robert. 1970. *Why Men Rebel.* Princeton: Princeton University Press.

———. 1993. *Minorities at Risk: A Global View of Ethnopolitical Conflicts.* Washington, D.C.: United States Institute of Peace Press.

Haghayeghi, Mehrdad. 1997. "Privatization Process in Kyrgyzstan." *Caspian Crossroads* 3 (Winter):24–26.

Halliday, Fred. 1974. *Arabia Without Sultans.* Harmondsworth: Penguin Books.

Hannum, Hurst. 1998. "The Specter of Secession." *Foreign Affairs* 77 (March/April):13–18.

Helms, Christine Moss. 1984. *Iraq: Eastern Flank of the Arab World.* Washington, D.C.: Brookings Institution.

Hough, Jerry. 1990. *Russia and the West: Gorbachev and the Politics of Reform,* 2nd ed. New York: Simon & Schuster.

Howard, Michael. 1995. "1945–1995: Reflections on Half a Century of British Security Policy." *International Affairs* 71:705–715.

Hsu, Immanuel C. Y. 1970. *The Rise of Modern China.* New York: Oxford University Press.

Huntington, Samuel P. 1991. *The Third Wave: Democratization in the Late Twentieth Century.* Norman: University of Oklahoma Press.

———. 1996. "Democracy for the Long Haul." *Journal of Democracy* 7 (April):3–13.

"In Search of Spring: A Survey of Russia." 1997. *The Economist,* July 12, S1–S18.

"Islam and the Ballot Box." 1997. *The Economist,* May 31, 41–42.

Jentleson, Bruce W. 1992. "The Pretty Prudent Public: Post Post–Vietnam American Opinion on the Use of Military Force." *International Studies Quarterly* 36:49–74.

Johnson, Chalmers A. 1962. *Peasant Nationalism and Communist Power: The Emergence of Revolutionary China, 1937–1945.* Stanford: Stanford University Press.

Jones, Stephen E. 1996. "Georgia's Return from Chaos." *Current History.* 95:340–345.

Juergensmeyer, Mark. 1993. *The New Cold War? Religious Nationalism Confronts the Secular State.* Berkeley: University of California Press.

Karabell, Zachary. 1996–97. "Fundamental Misconceptions: Islamic Foreign Policy." *Foreign Policy,* no. 105 (Winter):77–90.

Katz, Mark N. 1982. *The Third World in Soviet Military Thought.* Baltimore: Johns Hopkins University Press.

———. 1993. "The Legacy of Empire in International Relations." *Comparative Strategy* 12:365–383.

———. 1997. *Revolutions and Revolutionary Waves.* New York: St. Martin's Press.

Keatinge, Patrick. 1983. "Ireland: Neutrality Inside NPC." In *National Foreign Policies and European Political Cooperation,* edited by Christopher Hill, pp. 137–152. London: Royal Institute of International Affairs/George Allen & Unwin.

[Kennan, George F.] Mr. X. 1947. "The Sources of Soviet Conduct." *Foreign Affairs* 25 (July):566–82.

Kennedy, Paul. 1987. *The Rise and Fall of the Great Powers: Economic Change and Military Conflict from 1500 to 2000.* New York: Vintage Books.

Kerr, Malcolm H. 1971. *The Arab Cold War: Gamal 'Abd al-Nasir and His Rivals, 1958–1970,* 3rd ed. London: Oxford University Press.

Kirkpatrick, Jeane. 1979. "Dictatorships and Double Standards." *Commentary* 68 (November):34–45.

Knutsen, Torbjørn L. 1997. *A History of International Relations Theory,* 2nd ed. Manchester: Manchester University Press.

Knutsen, Torbjørn L., and Jennifer L. Bailey. 1989. "Over the Hill? The Anatomy of Revolution at Fifty." *Journal of Peace Research* 26: 421–431.

Kolakowski, Leszek. 1978. *Main Currents of Marxism: Its Rise, Growth, and Dissolution:* vol. 1, *The Founders;* vol. 2, *The Golden Age;* vol. 3, *The Breakdown.* Oxford: Oxford University Press.

Kristof, Nicholas. 1998. "Indonesia Struggles to Find New Reasons to Stay Intact." *New York Times,* May 24, pp. 1, 8.

Laroui, Abdallah. 1967. *L'idéologie arabe contemporaine.* Paris: François Maspero.

———. 1976. *The Crisis of the Arab Intellectual: Traditionalism or Historicism?* Berkeley: University of California Press.

Layachi, Azzedine. 1994. "Algerian Crisis, Western Choices." *Middle East Quarterly* 1 (September):55–62.

Lenczowski, George. 1980. *The Middle East in World Affairs,* 4th ed. Ithaca, NY: Cornell University Press.

Livy. 1960. *The Early History of Rome.* [Books I–V of *The History of Rome from its Foundation*]. Trans. Aubrey de Selincourt. Harmondsworth: Penguin Books.

———. 1982. *Rome and Italy.* [Books VI–X of *The History of Rome from its Foundation*]. Trans. Betty Radice. Harmondsworth: Penguin Books.

Lomperis, Timothy J. 1996. *From People's War to People's Rule: Insurgency, Intervention, and the Lessons of Vietnam.* Chapel Hill: University of North Carolina Press.

Low, D. A. 1991. *Eclipse of Empire.* Cambridge: Cambridge University Press.

MacFarlane, S. Neil. 1985. *Superpower Rivalry and Third World Radicalism: The Idea of National Liberation.* London: Croom Helm.

———. 1990. "Successes and Failures in Soviet Policy toward Marxist Revolutions in the Third World, 1917–1985." In *The USSR and Marxist Revolutions in the Third World,* edited by Mark N. Katz, pp. 6–50. Cambridge: Cambridge University Press.

Machiavelli, Niccolò. 1970. *The Discourses.* Ed. Bernard Crick. Harmondsworth: Penguin Books.

Markoff, John. 1996. *Waves of Democracy: Social Movements and Political Change.* Thousand Oaks, CA: Pine Forge Press.

Markus, Ustina. 1996. "Imperial Understretch: Belarus's Union with Russia." *Current History* 95:335–339.

Matlock, Jack. 1995. *Autopsy of an Empire: The American Ambassador's Account of the Collapse of the Soviet Union.* New York: Random House.

McCauley, Martin. 1993. *The Soviet Union, 1917–1991,* 2nd ed. London: Longman.

McDaniel, Tim. 1991. *Autocracy, Modernization, and Revolution in Russia and Iran*. Princeton: Princeton University Press.

"Mexico Enters the Era of Politics." 1997. *The Economist*, July. 12, 27–28.

Moore, Barrington, Jr. 1966. *Social Origins of Dictatorship and Democracy: Lord and Peasant in the Making of the Modern World*. Boston: Beacon Press.

Morgan, Dan, and David B. Ottaway. 1997. "U.S. Won't Bar Pipeline Across Iran." *Washington Post*, July 27, pp. A1, A27.

Morgenthau, Hans J. 1973. *Politics Among Nations: The Struggle for Power and Peace*, 5th ed. New York: Alfred A. Knopf.

Munson, Henry, Jr. 1988. *Islam and Revolution in the Middle East*. New Haven: Yale University Press.

Murphy, Richard W. 1997. "It's Time to Reconsider the Shunning of Iran." *Washington Post*, July 20, pp. C1, C6.

Nahaylo, Bohdan, and Victor Swoboda. 1990. *Soviet Disunion: A History of the Nationalities Problem in the USSR*. New York: Free Press.

Nasser, Gamal Abdul. 1955. *Egypt's Liberation: The Philosophy of the Revolution*. Washington, D.C.: Public Affairs Press.

Nkrumah, Kwame. [1957] 1971. *Ghana: The Autobiography of Kwame Nkrumah*. New York: International Publishers.

Noland, Marcus. 1997. "Why North Korea Will Muddle Through." *Foreign Affairs* 76 (July/August):105–118.

Ochs, Michael. 1997. "Turkmenistan: The Quest for Stability and Control." In *Conflict, Cleavage, and Change in Central Asia and the Caucasus*, edited by Karen Dawisha and Bruce Parrott, pp. 312–359. Cambridge: Cambridge University Press.

Olcott, Martha Brill. 1997. "Democratization and the Growth of Political Participation in Kazakstan." In *Conflict, Cleavage, and Change in Central Asia and the Caucasus*, edited by Karen Dawisha and Bruce Parrott, pp. 201–241. Cambridge: Cambridge University Press.

Ottaway, David. 1996. "Wielding Aid, U.S. Targets Sudan." *Washington Post*, November 10, p. A34.

Overholt, William H. 1996. "China after Deng." *Foreign Affairs* 75 (May/June):63–78.

Palmer, David Scott. 1996. "'Fujipopulism' and Peru's Progress." *Current History* 95:70–75.

Papp, Daniel S. 1985. *Soviet Perceptions of the Developing World in the 1980s: The Ideological Basis*. Lexington, MA: Lexington Books.

Petro, Nicolai N., and Alvin Z. Rubinstein. 1997. *Russian Foreign Policy: From Empire to Nation-State*. New York: Longman.

Pike, Douglas. 1987. *Vietnam and the Soviet Union: Anatomy of an Alliance.* Boulder, CO: Westview Press.

Pipes, Richard. 1997. "Is Russia Still an Enemy?" *Foreign Affairs* 76 (September/October):65–78.

"Retreat of Egypt's Islamists." 1997. *The Economist,* July 26, 37–38.

Robinson, Thomas W. 1989. "The Soviet Union and East Asia." In *The Limits of Soviet Power in the Developing World,* edited by Edward A. Kolodziej and Roger E. Kanet, pp. 171–199. Baltimore: Johns Hopkins University Press.

Rodman, Peter W. 1994. *More Precious Than Peace: The Cold War and the Struggle for the Third World.* New York: Charles Scribner's Sons.

Rosenthal, Andrew. 1991. "In Bush's Councils, a Growing Distrust of Yeltsin." *New York Times,* September 2, p. A7.

Roy, Olivier. 1994. *The Failure of Political Islam.* Cambridge, MA: Harvard University Press.

Ruehl, Lothar. 1992. "Limits of Leadership: Germany." In *From Occupation to Cooperation: The United States and United Germany in a Changing World Order,* edited by Steven Muller and Gebhard Schweigler, pp. 89–113. New York: W.W. Norton & Co.

Salloum, Habeeb. 1995. "Newfoundland—Canada's Come-by-Late Province." *Contemporary Review* 267:225–229.

Sasae, Kenichiro. 1994. *Rethinking Japan-U.S. Relations.* Adelphi Paper no. 292. London: International Institute for Strategic Studies.

Schmitter, Philippe C. 1995. "The International Context of Contemporary Democratization." In *Transitions to Democracy: Comparative Perspectives from Southern Europe, Latin America and Eastern Europe,* edited by Geoffrey Pridham, pp. 499–532. Aldershot, UK: Dartmouth.

Sederberg, Peter C. 1994. *Fires Within: Political Violence and Revolutionary Change.* New York: Harper Collins.

Selbin, Eric. 1998. "Same as It Ever Was: The Future of Revolution at the End of the Century." Paper presented at the International Studies Association Annual Convention, Minneapolis, March 21.

Serfaty, Simon. 1996–97. "Algeria Unhinged: What Next? Who Cares? Who Leads?" *Survival* 38(Winter):137–153.

Shambaugh, David. 1994. "Growing Strong: China's Challenge to Asian Security." *Survival* 36(Summer):43–59.

Sick, Gary. 1986. *All Fall Down: America's Tragic Encounter with Iran.* New York: Penguin Books.

Skocpol, Theda. 1979. *States and Social Revolutions: A Comparative Analysis of France, Russia, and China.* Cambridge: Cambridge University Press.

———. 1994. *Social Revolutions in the Modern World.* Cambridge: Cambridge University Press.

Slider, Darrell. 1997. "Democratization in Georgia." In *Conflict, Cleavage, and Change in Central Asia and the Caucasus,* edited by Karen Dawisha and Bruce Parrott, pp. 156–198. Cambridge: Cambridge University Press.

Smith, Gordon B. 1992. *Soviet Politics: Struggling with Change,* 2nd ed. New York: St. Martin's Press.

Smith, Tony. 1994. *America's Mission: The United States and the Worldwide Struggle for Democracy in the Twentieth Century.* Princeton: Princeton University Press.

Stone, Bailey. 1994. *The Genesis of the French Revolution: A Global-Historical Interpretation.* Cambridge: Cambridge University Press.

Svec, Milan. 1992. "Czechoslovakia's Velvet Divorce." *Current History* 91:376–380.

Tolz, Vera. 1996. "The War in Chechnya." *Current History* 95:316–321.

Treadgold, Donald W. 1990. *Twentieth Century Russia,* 7th ed. Boulder, CO: Westview Press.

Trueheart, Charles. 1997. "For Islanders of Former French Colony, Freedom Isn't All It's Cracked Up to Be." *Washington Post,* August 8, p. A26.

Tucker, Robert C., ed. 1975. *The Lenin Anthology.* New York: W. W. Norton.

Van Ness, Peter. 1970. *Revolution and Chinese Foreign Policy: Peking's Support for Wars of National Liberation.* Berkeley: University of California Press.

Walt, Stephen M. 1996. *Revolution and War.* Ithaca, NY: Cornell University Press.

White, Stephen, *et al.* 1997. *How Russia Votes.* Chatham, NJ: Chatham House Publishers.

Wickham-Crowley, Timothy P. 1992. *Guerrillas and Revolutions in Latin America: A Comparative Study of Insurgents and Regimes Since 1956.* Princeton: Princeton University Press.

Wiles, Peter. 1985. "Irreversibility: Theory and Practice." *The Washington Quarterly* 8 (Winter):29–40.

Yavlinsky, Grigory. 1998. "Russia's Phony Capitalism." *Foreign Affairs* 77 (May/June):67–79.

Yayla, Atilla. 1997. "Erbakan's Goals." *Middle East Quarterly* 4 (September):19–25.

Yinger, J. Milton. 1994. *Ethnicity: Source of Strength? Source of Conflict?* Albany: State University of New York Press.

Zakaria, Fareed. 1997. "The Rise of Illiberal Democracy." *Foreign Affairs* 76 (November/December):22–43.

INDEX